Women Leaders in Higher Education

In Western democratic countries, the feminization of the paid labour force has been one of the more important social and economic changes of the twentieth century. These changes heralded profound cultural challenges to expectations of women's social, political and economic participation and stimulated widespread debate about gender equity for women in education and employment across the public and private sectors. However, the significant under-representation of women in senior leadership roles in higher education remains.

Drawing extensively on narratives from women leaders and their female colleagues, the author examines the everyday experiences of women in senior leadership roles in an environment in which White women are a numerical minority and Indigenous women are a rare presence. These stories are not about triumph over adversity; they trace the ambiguities, contradictions, pleasures and ambivalences that women leaders experience. Importantly, the author brings into sharp relief the difficult and complicated territory that exists between women leaders and their female colleagues. This has the potential to produce a dissonance between how leaders view themselves and how they are viewed.

Women Leaders in Higher Education will be essential reading for anyone involved or interested in higher education policy and management, academic leadership, organizational diversity and gender studies.

Tanya Fitzgerald is Professor of Educational Leadership, Management and History at La Trobe University, Melbourne.

The Society for Research into Higher Education (SRHE) is an independent and financially self-supporting international learned Society. It is concerned to advance understanding of higher education, especially through the insights, perspectives and knowledge offered by systematic research and scholarship.

The Society's primary role is to improve the quality of higher education through facilitating knowledge exchange, discourse and publication of research. SRHE members are worldwide and the Society is an NGO in operational relations with UNESCO.

The Society has a wide set of aims and objectives. Amongst its many activities the Society:

● is a specialist publisher of higher education research, journals and books, amongst them Studies in Higher Education, Higher Education Quarterly, Research into Higher Education Abstracts and a long running monograph book series.

The Society also publishes a number of in-house guides and produces a specialist series "Issues in Postgraduate Education".

● funds and supports a large number of special interest networks for researchers and practitioners working in higher education from every discipline. These networks are open to all and offer a range of topical seminars, workshops and other events throughout the year ensuring the Society is in touch with all current research knowledge.

● runs the largest annual UK-based higher education research conference and parallel conference for postgraduate and newer researchers. This is attended by researchers from over 35 countries and showcases current research across every aspect of higher education.

SRHE

Society for Research into Higher Education
Advancing knowledge Informing policy Enhancing practice

73 Collier Street   T   +44 (0)20 7427 2350
London N1 9BE   F   +44 (0)20 7278 1135
United Kingdom   E   srheoffice@srhe.ac.uk

www.srhe.ac.uk

Director: Helen Perkins
Registered Charity No.313850
Company No. 00868820
Limited by Guarantee
Registered office as above

Society for Research into Higher Education (SRHE) series

Series Editor: Lynn McAlpine, Oxford Learning Institute
Jeroen Huisman, University of Bath

Published titles:
Intellectual Leadership in Higher Education: Renewing the Role of the University Professor
Bruce Macfarlane

Strategic Curriculum Change: Global Trends in Universities
Paul Blackmore and Camille B. Kandiko

Reconstructing Identities in Higher Education: The Rise of "Third Space" Professionals
Celia Whitchurch

The University in Dissent: Scholarship in the Corporate University
Gary Rolfe

Everything for Sale? The Marketisation of UK Higher Education
Roger Brown with Helen Carasso

Literacy in the Digital University: Learning as Social Practice in a Digital World
Robin Goodfellow and Mary R. Lea

Forthcoming titles:
Researching Student Learning in Higher Education: A Social Realist Approach
Jennifer M. Case

Women Leaders in Higher Education

Education

Shattering the myths

Tanya Fitzgerald

Routledge
Taylor & Francis Group

LONDON AND NEW YORK

First published 2014
by Routledge
2 Park Square, Milton Park, Abingdon, Oxon OX14 4RN
together with the Society for Research into Higher Education
73 Collier Street
London N1 9BE
UK

Simultaneously published in the USA and Canada
by Routledge
711 Third Avenue, New York, NY 10017 together with the
Society for Research into Higher Education
73 Collier Street
London N1 9BE
UK

Routledge is an imprint of the Taylor & Francis Group, an informa business

British Library Cataloguing in Publication Data
A catalogue record for this book is available from the British
Library

Library of Congress Cataloging in Publication Data
Catalog record for this book has been applied for

ISBN: 978-0-415-83489-6 (hbk)
ISBN: 978-0-415-83490-2 (pbk)
ISBN: 978-0-203-49151-5 (ebk)

Typeset in Galliard
by Wearset Ltd, Boldon, Tyne and Wear

MIX
Paper from
responsible sources
FSC
www.fsc.org   FSC® C013056

Printed and bound in Great Britain by
TJ International Ltd, Padstow, Cornwall

To the memory and legacy of
Mary Clare Gabrielle Holmes-Kinsella

11 August 1931–19 July 2009

Contents

Series editors' introduction

This series, co-published by the Society for Research into Higher Education and Routledge Books, aims to provide, in an accessible manner, cutting-edge scholarly thinking and inquiry that reflects the rapidly changing world of higher education, examined in a global context.

Encompassing topics of wide international relevance, the series includes every aspect of the international higher education research agenda, from strategic policy formulation and impact to pragmatic advice on best practice in the field. Each book in the series aims to meet at least one of the principal aims of the Society: to advance knowledge; to enhance practice; to inform policy.

The central theme of this book explores how women have negotiated and claimed a space for themselves in higher education. Based on empirical research carried out in Australia and New Zealand, Tanya Fitzgerald explores how women act in this space as leaders and managers. She vividly illustrates and analyses the ambiguities, silences and contradictions of women's lived leadership. The book ends on a positive note, arguing that women – although confronted with many challenges – can change university leadership, hierarchies and cultures.

Lynn McAlpine
Jeroen Huisman

Acknowledgements

This book is deeply embedded in my own academic and personal world. Although I am the author, I could not have produced this book without the assistance and support of a number of strong and vibrant women colleagues and friends. My sincere thanks go to all the women who participated in the research project for their willingness to share their stories. To Jane Grant, the research assistant who conducted a number of interviews, my thanks for your energy and commitment to the project. The assistance of Natasha Katoa in shaping and organizing the transcripts has been invaluable. Financial assistance from the Faculty of Education at La Trobe University for the data collection as well as a semester of research leave in 2012 provided much needed resources and time. To Elizabeth Smyth, my thanks for your hospitality during my visit to Canada. Your wise counsel is always so timely and most welcomed. I would also like to acknowledge Shannon Kerrigan and her ongoing interest in my work and willingness to agitate for change for and on behalf of women. Importantly, Eda Salvatore has kept me grounded as a leader with her salient advice and guidance. To the team at Routledge, I am grateful for seeing the potential in the book proposal and the professional advice and guidance that has been offered. I remain most indebted to Helen Gunter whose friendship I cherish for its intellectual stimulation, its reciprocity and its abiding warmth. And finally, to Ross Fitzgerald who truly knows the pain and joy behind the words, and has given so much – *e iti noa ana, na te aroha*.

Chapter 1

Telling lives

The intention in this book is to uncover the significant contribution of women as senior leaders in universities across Australia and New Zealand. Drawing on narratives from 30 women I examine *why* women seek to be leaders and *how* they enact leadership. Importantly, this book draws on the perspectives of 25 women colleagues that provide a nuanced understanding of the complexities and ambiguities women leaders face. This opening chapter introduces the reader to the challenges this book offers to the field, overviews the use of narrative to explore everyday experiences and outlines the central concerns that the book will traverse.

Introduction

In 1931 Virginia Woolf addressed members of the London and National Society for Women's Service. A well-known literary figure and established scholar, Woolf mused on her own biography and used the metaphor of a room of one's own to underscore the challenges women faced in their professional lives:

> You have won rooms of your own in the house hitherto exclusively owned by men, You are able, though not without great labour and effort to pay the rent.... But this freedom is only a beginning; the room is your own, but it is still bare.
>
> (Woolf 1957: chapter 27)

In her closing remarks, Woolf encouraged the audience to consider how they might furnish the room, with whom they might share it and under what terms. Based on a series of lectures, 'Women and Fiction', that she delivered in October 1928 at Newnham College and Girton College, two women's colleges at the University of Cambridge, *A Room of One's Own* draws together the central ideas. Woolf's proposition was that while women may face a number of limitations based on their gender, they should be given opportunity to be creative and independent. Her insistent plea is for women to have the freedom to venture into public spaces and to be able to develop their own capabilities. *A*

Room of One's Own is also about the fiction women write as well as the fiction written about women (Barrett 1979). Woolf's words are a backdrop to the stories of women leaders that filter through the chapters of this book. These stories are forms of autobiographical discourses that reveal aspects of women's professional lives. Containing details of women's lives, anxieties and triumphs, these stories are deeply personal.

Having a room of one's own is about the personal spaces that women occupy. The room or rooms that women call their own are furnished with their own books and memorabilia. These rooms can be places of solitude in which beliefs and behaviours can be formulated and examined. The suggestion in Woolf's work is that having a room or space of one's own is a pre-condition to speaking one's own mind, particularly within an environment that is both known and safe. In much the same way that Woolf uses the voice of another to express her views in *A Room of One's Own*, my voice is used in this book not to distance myself from the participants or audience, but as a way to enter into a conversation about the spaces and rooms that women leaders occupy. And like Woolf, as a narrator I stand between the readers and the participants, or characters in the stories I recall and recount.

In similar ways to Woolf's own writings, there is a connection in this book between speaker, narrator and reader. Following Woolf's example I do not play the 'hostess' and offer polite and conciliatory stories. Neither do I overlook the negative stories told about women leaders from the view of their female colleagues. Hence, I present a collection of observations in order to secure 'the greatest release of all ... which is the freedom to think of things in themselves' (Woolf 1957: chapter 39).

A Room of One's Own suggests that women occupy spaces as solitary inhabitants or that the room is one of many in a house where others are present. Drawing on this metaphor, I suggest that women leaders occupy rooms (offices) as leaders and managers in an institution (house) in which the majority of academic occupants are male. But it is in these spaces that women undertake a great deal of labour and emotional toil and, despite decades of affirmative action strategies and equity legislation, still struggle to claim a leadership space as their own. However, the academic house will remain bare until numerical imbalances are remedied and more inclusive institutional cultures emerge. The diversity of space that Woolf alludes to is notably absent across institutions of higher education. In this book my interest lies in uncovering ways in which women have negotiated and claimed a space for themselves in higher education, and how, once in this space, they act as leaders and managers.

The 30 senior women and 25 academic women whose voices trickle through the chapters of this book have generously shared their stories – stories that are infused with anger, laughter, pleasure and raw emotion. The women are all very aware of their privileged position at the apex of the academic hierarchy and many consider they 'pave the way for those who come behind us' (Aroha, Indigenous academic). Intensely mindful that their colleagues across the sector look to them for advice, guidance, support and mentoring, a number of the senior women leaders are conscious of a mandate to 'be unruly, to transgress boundaries and… unpick power relations and see what happens, what can be restructured and deconstructed' (Kathleen, senior leader SL).

My intentions are twofold; to examine the everyday experiences of women in senior leadership roles in higher education, and to explore the perceptions of their female colleagues. These intentions echo the work of Sinclair and Wilson (2002) who suggest that leaders and leadership are constructed in the minds of their audience. This has the potential to produce a dissonance between how leaders view themselves and how they are viewed. Women are acutely aware that their performance as leaders is frequently perceived, presented and viewed differently from that of men (Avis 2002; Blackmore 1997; Deem 2004). Such perceptions are based on gendered stereotypes and expectations of what is '[in]appropriate behaviour for women and men leaders'. Indeed 'a woman leader is not viewed as androgynous or undifferentiated from her male counterparts. She is viewed as a woman who is a leader' (Adler 1999: 259).

The emphasis is on making audible the voices and experiences of women leaders in universities across Australia and New Zealand. Although I draw on examples from these two settings, the issues and experiences surfaced are not uncommon across Western institutions of higher education (see for example Allan 2008; Bagilhole and White 2011; Cotterill *et al.* 2007; Sagaria 2007). Despite local variations, common struggles for women include establishing boundaries around work–life balance, securing promotion and recognition, balancing career expectations and choices, negotiating high teaching and administrative loads, meeting demands of research audits (Hazelkorn 2011) and negotiations in and around the gendered cultures of higher education (Currie *et al.* 2002).

A common thread across the literatures and contexts is the varying impacts of institutional cultures that inspire or restrict women leaders. In the words of Noelle, one of the senior women participants, 'it is important to show how women leaders lead and act in the quiet spaces' and 'create opportunities for women to think about what is possible and permissible'. This is about creating room for women's voices to be heard (Fitzgerald 2010; Marshall 1995) and their leadership lives to be made more visible.

The impetus for the project and book originate in my own career trajectory and leadership work. My experiences as a feminist academic have spoken to me about the joys and rewards of a scholarly career as well as the isolation and loneliness of leadership roles in the academy, particularly for women. I have worked in four universities across three countries as well as in a corporate company. In all of these settings I have occupied formal leadership roles and all of my managers have been women. Frequently too I have felt like an outsider. First, this has originated from my being a scholarly immigrant to a new culture, a new institution and a new country. Second, this has been due to the marked absence of women in mid-senior positions in the places I have found myself. I have frequently attended meetings in which the majority of participants are male and at times the only two women present have been the committee secretary and myself. Third, I have been an outsider as the previous incumbent in each university, occupational role and geographical location has been male. In three of the settings, I have been the first woman in that department or school to take on a leadership role. This brief career vignette speaks to the different rooms I have occupied and how I have sought to furnish each in particular ways and at particular moments.

Being a leader as Noelle (SL) suggested is about creating a different space. And like Virginia Woolf, it is about creating a space for women to transgress, to cross into spaces that she has not been previously permitted to enter, and in that space to realize her capabilities. Helen's (SL) comments speak to the spaces that leaders are required to occupy:

> When you apply for a job as a lecturer or senior lecturer, the emphasis, the questions and the PD [position description] is all about you. All about what you might bring to the place. But when you apply for a senior management job, it's all about what you can do for others. What you are prepared to do for others and how you are going to bring about the change that is needed.

Helen's words here highlight the extent to which leaders are situated in relation to others. And it is from this relationship that leadership can be simultaneously pleasurable and painful. Leadership can, and does, consume time, energy and emotions. In the current managerial climate of higher education, leaders are expected to act as autonomous self-regulating and self-maximizing individuals (Blackmore and Sachs 2007; Davies *et al.* 2006) yet they are defined in relation to those they lead. Accordingly, these relationships and perceptions are important to interrogate in order to think more broadly about leaders and leadership.

My purpose from the outset is to complicate 'leadership' and tease out the ambiguities, silences and contradictions of women's lived leadership lives. I do not wish to solidify prevailing assumptions about women's conscious and unconscious leadership work (see for example Coleman 2011; Glazer-Raymo 2008), but examine *why* they seek to be leaders and *how* they enact leadership.

In numerous ways, this book is a departure from thinking about leadership as a set of personal attributes to thinking about leadership as relational. An uneasy tension that I bring to the surface is the recognition that women do not always exercise leadership in positive and self-affirming ways. Not all women in senior roles have paved the way for their female colleagues. As Gini (2001: 99) explains 'having achieved success by playing hardball and working hard, they [women] expect the same from others'. It is possible that institutional climates that legitimate aggressiveness, competitiveness and autonomy (Collinson and Hearn 1994, 1996) through promotion, recognition and reward systems create rivalries between women colleagues (Miner and Longino 1987). Or is it the case that some women have successfully assimilated to these ways of working?

Within this inhospitable atmosphere, instead of laying the groundwork for the advancement of their female colleagues (Mavin 2006), women are less than positive role models. In some instances, women are perceived by their female colleagues to abuse leadership. But as I disclose, this abuse might rest on flawed assumptions of collegiality and support from women at senior levels as well as unrealistic expectations that women who have broken through the glass ceiling (Davidson and Cooper 1992; Liff and Ward 2001) will inevitably represent the interests of all women. Furthermore, women can be labelled queen bees (Mavin 2008) if they either act or fail to act in gendered ways. Competing expectations and anticipations about women leaders from both female and male colleagues can create leadership as an almost untenable space for women.

As a strategy for survival women leaders can adopt internalized masculinist practices (Collinson and Hearn 1996; Connell 1995) and are consequently perceived as oppositional by their peers and colleagues. Those women who do talk the language of managerialism shatter any myths surrounding the 'woman leader' and can open themselves up for rebuke and criticism precisely because they do not operate in gendered ways. The backlash against women who seek power in institutions is not restricted to their male colleagues (Parks-Stamm *et al.* 2008). Women leaders can face vertical and horizontal oppression from their female colleagues as well as engage in a level of aggression themselves. Being a leader is risky work.

Dangerous terrain

The introduction of managerialism and managerial practices has created a new level of workers within higher education (Morley 2001), the manager-academic (Deem 2003), many of whom are women. In a devolved system where risk and responsibility are located at the school/department level this is dangerous terrain for women as they bear the burden for ensuring that performance indicators are met, compliance secured, financial viability and profitability enhanced and the student experience improved. In these roles women are required to act as change agents as well as managers of the increasingly corporate culture of the university. The intolerable and unrelenting pressures of corporatized universities (Marginson 2000) require certain forms of leadership and management.

Managerialism encourages ownership of and participation in decision-making, the building of networks within and across institutions, a flexible and responsive approach to 'client' needs, innovative capabilities, relational skills and collaborative approaches to leadership. It is these supposedly soft skills that are increasingly promoted as women's ways of leading (Blackmore 1999; Due Billing and Alvesson 2000; Manning 2002). Images of being tough, entrepreneurial, decisive, flexible and self-interested are linked with being male and masculine (Acker 1990; Bradley 1999; Collinson and Hearn 1996).

Women who have been successful in obtaining senior roles are unable to openly discuss the discriminatory structures, attitudes or practices they encounter as they may well be labelled as troublemakers and provoke a structural backlash (Sinclair 1998). Parading women as a 'symbol and measure of organizational change' (Wajcman 1998: 2) might well be perceived as a threat to male and masculine power as well as providing ammunition for intolerant discourses that assert women are appointed to these roles because of their gender and not on merit.

I am troubled by assumptions that leadership can be reduced to an adjective or that there is a specific set of lenses through which leadership can be viewed. Populist feminized discourses suggest that women lead in 'softer' and more 'feminine' ways (Coleman 2011; Hall 1996). These universalizing and reductionist discourses make leadership for women difficult if not impossible. Depicted as essentially lacking hard skills, women are required to upgrade their skills in order to meet current leadership demands. This places women at risk because they are then cast as being 'one of the boys'. Being 'one of the boys' is a risky business as women can be subsequently located in token roles as they have 'failed' to meet the standards set by the benchmark men (Thornton 2000). Lynette (SL) observed that:

> there are females who tend more to the masculine side and if that is what they are doing they are going to get the blokey blokes particularly off side. I do believe there are differences in the way males and females lead, construct themselves, think of themselves … the interesting thing is when it doesn't work and you are playing by your rules as a female leader they don't know that game. It is very difficult to play a game if you don't know what the rules are, that can really be a very interesting tussle.

Being too similar to the 'blokey blokes' was seen by Lynette as a way to provoke a level of opposition. Women who 'play a different game', that is, act in feminine ways, are in a difficult position as the 'blokes' neither know the game nor understand the rules. Wajcman (1998: 7) contends that 'women's presence in the world of men is conditional on them being willing to modify their behaviour to become more like men or to be perceived as more male than men'. This can be seen in the comments offered by Lillian (SL):

> I do think they [women] face this blokey culture that can develop, and the banter and the kind of in-club that can form. That can be as equally threatening for the non-blokey bloke as it can be for some women. I know men who feel just as alienated as women. In academia there is that potential for it to be a very blokey culture. The statistics tell us that. Trying to overcome this blokey culture is almost impossible.

When a woman behaves as a leader and exercises authority, it implicitly suggests that women's leadership performance 'fits' and fits in. This obliges women to play a range of roles depending on the circumstances. Fundamentally women are a threat to the worldview of their male colleagues and must 'play the game' and 'learn the rules', that is, conform to the male worldview, accept their (limited) role, or be excluded for transgressing these boundaries (Fitzgerald 2012b).

According to Lynette (SL) 'a female way of playing the game is that you won't play the game – their game – because they want to play a political game which ties you in knots'. Lynette's refusal to play the game or communicate 'what the rules are' placed her simultaneously in a tentative and a liberating position. Her reluctance to 'play the game' exposed her lack of commitment to masculinized management styles and she could well be excluded from further participation in the world of what she termed the 'blokey bloke'. Her own political response to the situation was to devise her own rules; rules that she predicted would lead to 'a very interesting tussle' with her male colleagues. Both Lynette's and Lillian's narratives show that women spend a great deal of time and energy engaged in the process of self-analysis about what it means to 'lead' and be a 'leader'. Both attempted to find a comfortable space for themselves as women and as leaders despite the complexities and uncertainties they faced as they attempted to collude with a game that was not of their making.

Margaret, a senior leader, remarked on the climate of competition and individualism (Metcalfe and Slaughter 2008) that she witnessed. 'I do see in male managers a lot of posturing and ego-driven behaviour' she said. 'I see empire building. It's not true of all of them but it is more common amongst men than it is amongst women.' This is the climate that is increasingly chilly for women (Maranto and Griffin 2011). Part of the reason for this chilly climate is that being male and masculine is the norm whereas being female is a default from this norm. A woman participant commented on the subtle yet persistent operation of gender that she had witnessed:

> I recall sitting in a meeting recently. The male chair kept urging the membership to 'speak to the Dean, he is the one to lobby'. Now at this university there are two women Deans. So I kept saying 'she' every time only he was referred to. But it didn't stop, he just did not get the message. But I kept on at him. I was a niggling echo. After about the fifth time he just stopped talking and glared at me. I held his stare.
>
> (Alana, SL)

This example speaks to the everyday experiences of numbers of women in organizations who work to remind their colleagues that it is not only men who occupy powerful positions (Wajcman 1998; Whitehead 1998). Being female or being male entails differing experiences of reality and although each is exposed to the same world, they differently mediate the way in which their relationship with that world is socially constructed. Recounting that world is a form of social practice through which knowledge is preserved and transmitted (Gherardi 1996). To this end, I present stories of women leaders in the largely male setting of senior university administration as a way to show their realities with/ in the spaces they occupy. The example embedded in Alana's story (above) is not just about the continual struggle of women to be recognized. It is also an example of how men remain caught in a gender trap; that they anticipate that being male and masculine is the norm.

Feminist women leaders are themselves at risk both personally and professionally as they seek to challenge the status quo and unsettle what is perceived as the 'natural order' of organizational life. Creating opportunities previously denied to their female colleagues and other equity groups is risky work. Keeping gender on the agenda can make the benchmark men (Thornton 2000) uncomfortable. 'Mention gender', said Kayla (SL), 'and the men in the room go very quiet. I think they think we have done gender... But don't mention it and nothing changes.' Gender work that is constituted as women's work acts to assure women that their needs, aspirations and desires are recognized. Yet this work is afforded less status due to the inherent nature of the care work that is required (Devine et al. 2011).

Part of a numerical minority (Bagilhole and White 2011; Morley 2013), senior women are in a decidedly precarious position as their performance as managers is highly scrutinized by their colleagues. Any failure to respond to institutional demands and external accountabilities can expose women to high levels of rebuke and criticism (Ryan et al. 2007). The reflections offered by Helen (SL) underscore this point:

> I came to this place because I wanted the job and I thought it would be a good career move. I expected it to be tough and that a great deal needed to be done. I was prepared for that. But I was not prepared for the loneliness. I am the only woman at this level, no one seems to understand what that means, the juggling that needs to go on just to get here in the mornings and then to stay way beyond the normal hours. The pressure is almost intolerable ... the pressure to get it right, and get it right the first time. Are they waiting for me to stumble and fail?

Indigenous women and ethnic minority women are hyper-visible (Fitzgerald 2010). Consequently these women are exposed to institutional scrutiny based on gender and ethnicity. They are frequently expected to engage in 'mammy work' (Collins 1998: 49) as well as the politics of identity and community (Essed 2000). Unlike their White female colleagues, Indigenous women and ethnic minority women carry the expectations of their communities and as academics face a triple burden of work; the organization, and family and traditional obligations (Chilisa and Ntseane 2010; Mama 2003). For White women, higher education can be an intensely lonely and hostile place, for Indigenous women, institutional climates can invoke further experiences of assimilation and marginalization (Battiste 2000; Moreton-Robinson 2000).

Insiders, outsiders or strangers?

Employment legislation and affirmative action strategies as well as a degree of internal focus on equity policies and equitable practices have the potential to challenge and change institutional structures and organizational cultures. Possibilities do exist for Indigenous women and ethnic minority women to agitate for change to the very policies, practices and discourses that marginalize and subordinate (Dace 2012; Fee and Russell 2007). A consequence any change to the status quo can prompt is that new organizational spaces that value relational skills, collegiality and collaborative ways of working are opened up. It is in these spaces that women can be insiders based on their skill sets rather than as outsiders based on their status as the organizational 'other' (Probert 2005). Yet even as insiders women can be constrained by their outside responsibilities.

Gherardi (1996) has commented that women in traditionally male occupations often experience the position of being outsiders on the inside and their experiences are as strangers entering a 'non-natural' culture. Frequently there is no one readily available to assist them in gaining access to the systems and institutional (inside) networks that are required for success (Bryson 2004; Gibson 2006). Indigenous women and ethnic minority women face a double positioning. They are outsiders to the environment that White women inhabit yet insiders based on their gender, and outsiders in academia based on exigencies of race, ethnicity and gender. In many ways they are peripheral participants in higher education. Lynne, an Indigenous academic, offered a poignant reminder of the institutional colonization that can occur:

> I never feel that I belong. I cannot connect with the people here. They don't come from where I do, they don't know even to ask where I come from or who I identify with. I hear my colleagues talk about how hard it is, how lonely it is to be the only woman in the role. It's double for me, I am lonely because I am not recognized, that who I am does not seem to matter. And I am lonely because I am a mother, sister, aunt and grandmother and no one knows that. This place is strange to me and I am a stranger to it.

Women leaders have a degree of institutional power and authority ostensibly based on their position and portfolio in the academic hierarchy. As such, they are insiders to the organizational bureaucracy and associated with the managerial career path. Predominantly located in institutional housekeeping roles, women are simultaneously part of the managerial fabric of the organization yet marginalized. On the basis of their gender they are outsiders to the masculinist culture that accentuates executive attributes (as opposed to scholarly attributes) such as tact, firmness, commitment, common sense, self-empowerment and assertiveness. Insider knowledge such as understanding the 'rules of the game' (Acker 2010; Goode and Bagilhole 1998) is a critical component of the leadership game. Hence, women leaders are risky intruders in the leadership game as they can actively work to disrupt the game and introduce their own rules (Eveline 2005; Meyerson and Tompkins 2007).

Women who are able to play the leadership game are less likely to be strangers as the more senior they become in the organization, the more likely it is that they will demonstrate the kinds of masculine behaviour required (Miller 2006). Becoming more of an insider to this culture potentially renders a woman as an outsider to her female colleagues which can produce a clash of expectations and perceptions between the roles of 'woman' and 'leader'. Thus, women are both outsiders on the inside and insiders on the outside. There is an incongruity here because if women deploy aspects of femininity to make themselves more caring managers they are performing to expectations (Acker 2012). But if they perform to the same expectations required of male leaders, they run the risk of being accused of adopting hegemonic masculine ways of leading (Mavin 2006). In contrast, male leaders who care are rewarded for their capacities to undertake such work (Connell 2006).

In many ways women cannot win. They face the contradictory demands of being feminine and business-like (Wajcman 1998) but once they begin to behave like men, they cannot be proper women (Maddock 1999). The adversarial nature of male norms such as controlling, competing, organizing, establishing rules and regulations and deferring to a higher authority (Gherardi and Poggio 2007; Schein and Davidson 1993) are not immediately part of women's leadership toolkits. Women are more likely to apply relational, collaborative and participatory skills (Sinclair 1998). On the one hand, women are criticized for their supposedly feminine qualities that do not match organizational male norms and, on the other, those who perform these managerial behaviours are reviled for being too masculine (Connell 2006; Kloot 2004). In order to 'fit in' (Bryans and Mavin 2003), women must lose their exaggerated visibility as well as distance themselves from a minority group, women colleagues, to win acceptance from majority men. How then do women understand and articulate their lives? What then of the women who disrupt organizational norms? And what are the observations of their female colleagues? These are the central questions that are addressed in this book.

Composing and narrating lives

The impetus for the research reported in this book was my own disquiet about the role and participation of women in higher education. Across a range of institutions in Australia and New Zealand, I have witnessed women evacuating senior roles and what appeared to be an unwillingness by their female colleagues to indicate they would consider a formal leadership role. In several locations I have observed the cultural backlash against feminist women in these positions. Not part of the 'boys' club', feminist women were seen as trouble; trouble primarily because they agitated for change and challenged masculinist practices. In the majority of cases the emotional toll was such that they left academia. Their male colleagues subsequently reclaimed the spaces women had vacated.

Echoing a silence in feminist writing, the women featured in this book were less likely to reflect on the pleasures they found in their work. Many had to reconcile being in a relatively powerful and visible position with their nurturing and egalitarian ideals. In many ways these women had to negotiate between what Gallop (1995) refers to as the 'good-girl feminist', the hard-working and caring female academic, and the 'bad-girl feminist', the female academic who took pleasure in positions of power and authority. But there are other stories to be told.

My interest lies in capturing the stories of women leaders, to understand their strategic negotiations and navigations, to consider the subtle yet insistent exclusion of women from senior ranks and to interrogate how women understand leadership. Due in part to my own disquiet, I wanted to investigate how women leaders supported, encouraged and nurtured their female colleagues and the extent to which observations similar to my own had encouraged or discouraged women from considering senior leadership positions. A level of discomfort surfaces principally because I do not wish to produce a text that suggests that women are complicit in their own demise or a text which prompts a structural and cultural backlash against women leaders.

The powerful potential of women's stories is that they offer a counternarrative about how women 'do and perform' leadership. Their stories highlight that leadership is contextual, personal and adaptive. That is, leadership is enacted in different ways according to circumstance, space and time. Women do not 'do and perform' leadership in uniform ways and their everyday experiences and practices are as varied as women themselves. I have woven women's narratives through the chapters to infuse the text with their everyday voices and experiences. Importantly these narratives highlight the pleasures, contradictions, rewards, challenges, negotiations, successes, exclusions and disappointments that women leaders have experienced at various times and in various ways.

The complexities and ambiguities of their lives as leaders were drawn from a research project that involved 55 women; of this group 30 identified themselves as senior women leaders and 25 were academic women. The 30 women occupied senior positions as deans (10), pro vice chancellors (PVC, 12) and deputy vice chancellors (DVC, 8). The majority of women (22) were in Australia. In total, 23 women were externally recruited and seven were promoted internally. All of the women had higher degrees and/or professional qualifications. All had worked in more than one institution across their careers and six of the women had worked in different countries. The majority held the title of professor (27) and three were associate professors in senior portfolios. Twelve of the women were known in their fields outside of the university as they sat on professional committees, research councils, school governing councils or community boards. All of the women were aged 50 years or over.

To understand the perceptions of academic women towards women leaders, 25 academic women were interviewed. Of this group, 15 were in Australia and

10 in New Zealand. In terms of demographic profile, their ages ranged from 35 to 67, they occupied roles as research assistants (2), associate lecturers (3), lecturers (11), senior lecturers (9). In this group, 18 women had PhD degrees and the remaining seven expected to submit within a short period of time. The majority of women worked in fields such as Humanities, Social Sciences and Public Health and had spent periods of time working in their own professional fields. Seven of the women had worked in more than one university and nine identified as Indigenous women. Each of the Indigenous women held leadership portfolios at middle management levels, portfolios linked with access and equity or Indigenous education. Importantly, narratives from the 25 academic women offer a distinctive lens through which to view the vitality and vibrancy of women's leadership. But I do not ignore the negative aspects of women's leadership. Neither do I offer a linear narrative nor attempt to universalize women or their leadership experiences.

I did not attempt to 'match' leaders with their university colleagues but sought to gather stories about various experiences. An immediate advantage was that the group of 30 senior women recounted their perceptions of women they had worked with in either the same or a previous institution. This broadened the narratives.

Fundamental to this project was the issue of confidentiality. As the academic community across Australia and New Zealand is relatively small and women a minority within these geographical boundaries, neither specific geographical locations nor institutions have been named. Pseudonyms as well as generalized terms are used to denote participants. Accordingly SL (senior leader) is used to denote participants at the level of dean, associate or deputy dean, PVC, or DVC levels. The term 'academic' is used to denote a female colleague. At the time of the interviews, while each of the women worked in a particular university they were asked to draw on their experiences and own perceptions across their careers. A deliberate decision was made to not interview women vice chancellors or chancellors; this executive level of leadership in the public sector will be a different project at a different time.

Intensive semi-structured interviews were undertaken to explore womens' perceptions, experiences and everyday realities of leadership. Invitations to participate were extended to senior women who were identified by their institutional titles and hierarchical location. Academic women were selected based on their individual university website profile that indicated disciplinary expertise, academic background and current role. All interviews were recorded and transcribed. Transcripts were subject to a complex and careful process of analysis designed to maximize understanding of the specificities of women's leadership lives. Using procedures common to interpretive analysis, transcripts were read and tentative categories or codes formulated. Each interview was abstracted and indexed according to themes developed through extensive literature reviews (see for example Fitzgerald 2010, 2012b; Fitzgerald and Wilkinson 2010).

Women's talk with women was a powerful methodological tool as it prompted a level of reciprocity within the interview as well as across a number of participants. This was one of the unintended consequences of this project; women met up with colleagues at cross-institutional meetings (such as the Innovative Universities meetings in Australia), seminars and conferences and openly talked about their participation. At my own university a number of women contribute to and attend the Senior Women's Network and discussed their involvement in this project as part of those meetings. Thus, experiences were shared beyond the project and women formed their own supportive alliances. Some 14 months after the conclusion of the formal data collection phase, women report that they still network with each other.

In general, interviews lasted longer than the intended 40 minutes; 18 were of two hours' duration. Those interviewed were keenly interested in the study and talked at length about their professional lives across a number of institutions. A research assistant conducted interviews with women in the institutions in which I had worked. In order to further protect their anonymity, their interview consent forms were given to me in a sealed envelope, all transcripts and verification of data were undertaken by the research assistant. Using the anonymized transcripts, I devised and interpreted the themes.

These data have been used to craft a narrative about how women make sense of their professional lives as leaders as well as the everyday ambiguities, complexities and dilemmas they encounter. In similar ways to Marshall's (1995) work on women leaders, direct quotes from interviews are used to illustrate womens' perceptions and experiences. Some of these quotes appear to be lengthy and uneven but a deliberate decision was made not to confine women's words and to allow the richness of their perspectives to surface. As I have witnessed, it is frequently in the 'spaces in-between' (Fitzgerald 2010) that the nuances of our lives can be revealed.

I am intensely mindful of the dangers of ethnocentric scholarship (Dace 2012; Fitzgerald 2010; Maher and Tetreault 2007; Rhode 2003) and the silences that frequently surround Indigenous women in the academy. This book rehabilitates some of these silences through the inclusion of their voices. In sharing their stories about the obstacles and barriers they face every day as Indigenous women, their desire was for their listeners and readers to acquire an understanding of the spaces they occupy and to begin a conversation about the possibilities cross-cultural alliances offer. Although their frustrations, disappointments and successes resonate with broader narratives, their stories highlight the extent to which the academy remains dangerous terrain for women of colour, Indigenous women and ethnic minority women to occupy. As Moana an Indigenous woman mused:

I feel like an outsider in the world of all academic men and my Pākehā [White] colleagues. I have learned to make choices about what I do and what I say. But my choices do not sit comfortably with me and I struggle to retain who I am.

These sentiments were echoed by Myra, an Indigenous academic:

> Applying for jobs ... it's hard ... it kind of gets you down ... you wonder if it is all worth it. I was encouraged to go for jobs ... but I found myself fighting on too many fronts.... White institutions, White men, White women even Indigenous men. I have to get past all of these, be better.

Doubly identified on the basis of gender and ethnicity, Indigenous and ethnic minority women are scarce in senior roles and identification can be difficult to mask. In order to respect individuality as well as de-identify these women, I use the term Indigenous women in this text. Although each of the nine Indigenous women interviewed began by telling me of their links with their land and family networks, this information is not provided for the reader as they are markers of identity and would render anonymity redundant. Broader terms such as Indigenous woman assist with the recognition of their identities but do not suggest a predisposition to a distinctive group consciousness (Collins 1991). Each of the women was adamant that she wanted to be part of the conversation about leadership in her own attempt to break the silences. Each of the Indigenous women interviewed had her own story to tell; and it was a story that detailed loss and longing as well as struggle and compromise. Importantly, narrating their stories provided participants with space to talk their truths rather than present the 'official' versions (Bishop 1998). This form of narrative inquiry offers a level of authenticity that resonates with Indigenous peoples (Battiste 2000; Fitzgerald 2010).

Linking to a range of family groups and ancestral lands, Indigenous women reflect on the complexities of their lives across location, dislocation, spirituality, gender and ethnicity. This text does not 'add on' Indigenous voices but seeks to offer an account of the lived realities of their lives and experiences in the academy. In much the same way that I do not universalize what it means to be a 'woman leader', nor do I assume that Indigenous women share the same interests or act in particular ways.

Immediately problematic is how to proceed epistemologically and methodologically without creating narratives of similarities and difference between women or between two specific locations. The resolution lies in creating space for multiple voices to be heard. There is no grand narrative to be told. The stories are not about triumph over adversity but they do trace the ambiguities, contradictions, pleasures and ambivalences that women leaders experience. I bring into sharp relief the local and specific circumstances of women's professional lives that are blended by broader global discourses circulating around higher education.

Globally, universities have been subject to workplace restructuring as a consequence of renewed managerial emphasis on accountability, productivity, financial longevity, commercialization, competition, internationalization, quality assurance and institutional performance (Davies *et al.* 2006; Deem and Brehony

2005; Slaughter and Rhoades 2004). Importantly, I play close attention to the gendered repercussions these changes have stimulated in two specific locations. But I do not offer a cross-national, cross-cultural, cross-disciplinary or cross-institutional analysis of womens' experiences. What I do develop is what Dorothy Smith (1990) refers to as a theorized narrative that reveals points of shared interest and opportunity. This permits a drawing out of local knowledge and voices as mirror images of what might be occurring elsewhere.

The work of Mary Bateson (1989), a writer and cultural anthropologist, has influenced decisions about how to present the everyday lives of women leaders. Her narrative study *Composing a Life* underscores the use of improvizational forms that recognize and celebrate complex lives that are fluid rather than linear, disrupted rather than continuous; lives that are 'continually refocused and redefined' (Bateson 1989: 9). Adopting the metaphor of 'composing a life', Bateson invites readers to see a life as 'improvisations, discovering the shape of our creation along the way, rather than pursuing a vision already defined' (Bateson 1989: 1). She further adds that:

> It is time to explore the creative potential of interrupted and conflicted lives, where energies are not narrowly focused or permanently pointed toward a single ambition.... Composing a life involves a continual reimagining of the future and reinterpretations of the past to give meaning to the present.
>
> (1989: 9, 29)

Bateson is advocating for reading lives as discontinuous and changeful experiences. But what she does not appear to acknowledge is the multiple and potentially conflicting voices that may emerge in any one narrative or across a set of narratives. Although the stories retold in this book do not necessarily go beyond career/life plots, they do underscore the complex and contradictory everyday experiences of women leaders.

In describing the lives of five women, Bateson uses words such as create, shape, define, combine, design, identify and identity to illustrate the evolving nature of individual lives. In traversing each of the women's personal and work lives, Bateson (1989: 237) deduces that:

> Our lives are full of surprises, for none of us has followed a specific ambition toward a specific goal. Instead, we have learned from interruptions and improvised from the materials that came to hand, reshaping and reinterpreting. As a result, all of us have lived with high levels of ambiguity.

Although published over 20 years ago, Bateson's notion of composing a life remains relevant particularly for women who are looking at how to identify themselves as leaders in a rapidly shifting environment such as higher education. 'These are not lives without commitment, but rather lives in which commitments are continually refocused and redefined' (Bateson 1989: 9). I am particularly drawn to the notion of lives that are flexible and adaptable and which are marked by intentional action and improvisation. The composition of women's lives in this book has been an iterative process; text has been crafted and recrafted so that patterns can be discovered and constructed. This narrative approach permits a patchwork of experiences, roles and identities to be discovered, shaped and created (Bateson 1989).

The storytelling approach that is adopted offered opportunities for women to recall and voice their experiences and observations. These are not smooth developmental stories but a series of vignettes of memory that do not follow any linear pattern. Many of the plotlines falter as women question their own abilities and knowledge and express their uncertainties about whether they are being changed or changing practices.

These constructed stories have some relation to the meaning attached to the past and may be more of a reflection of this meaning than a reflection of past reality (Richardson 1997). The self-presentation of these women is then a story about the choices they have made throughout their professional lives as well as a story about how they positioned themselves in the interview. Their selves and their work worlds reflect connections made between events, recall and meaning.

Interviews adopted a conversational style and a number of participants offered comments such as: 'I am not sure that I would be this candid with a male interviewer', or 'It helps to talk about all of this with a woman. I feel like I don't have to interpret my world.' Like Hall (1996), much of the material is presented in women's own words (autobiographical) as the text moves between stories of their actions (the everyday) and my own commentary. These narratives are artefacts through which institutional cultures can be framed, understood and interpreted and their dominant values and norms identified (Gherardi 2007). Furthermore, I scrutinize 'what' is recounted as well as 'how' women impose meaning on events, actions and individuals in their lives to show sequentiality and causality when women travel into and around male worlds (Bryans and Mavin 2003; Gherardi 1996). As highly successful women in senior roles each was in an extra-ordinary position; not only were they part of a numerical minority they were simultaneously observers of and participants in the rites, rules and practices of institutional cultures.

Overview

The title *Women Leaders in Higher Education: Shattering the Myths* sets the agenda for this book. Drawing on a range of literatures that have contributed to my understanding of the gendered construction of leadership and organizations, this book interrogates what it means to be a woman leader in contemporary higher education settings.

This book has resonance across the higher education sector as the market values that have swept across institutions on an international scale have led to a commonality of experience about what it now means to work in academia and be an academic. I acknowledge that institutions of higher education are located in nations with their own specific historical, cultural, social, economic, legal and political legacies that render comparisons difficult. However the subtle and pervasive global problem that remains is that women remain significantly under-represented at senior levels in higher education

In drawing together stories from women academics across Australia and New Zealand, this book speaks to the particular local experiences of White women and Indigenous women. This book speaks to an audience more globally as these stories reveal the diversity of women's institutionally situated experiences and 'fill in the detail' (Acker 1994: 147) that generalized broad narratives do not offer.

The research work and theorizing that are presented disrupt a number of narratives. There is neither a feminist fairy tale to be told about women and their leadership work nor a list of hints and tips for 'good practitioners' to be produced. Although narratives of women's life cycles as academics and leaders are presented, attention is paid to the dissonances and discontinuities. Differences in perceptions between women are presented to bring into sharp relief the difficult and complicated territory that exists between powerful and less powerful women. Significantly, this book seeks to reduce the privilege of White women's voices that can reproduce and intensify the monocultural narratives of the powerful (Fitzgerald 2010). Accordingly, the dual emphasis across the chapters lies in exposing the myths that surround 'women' as leaders in higher education and interrogating the silences that exist.

In Chapter 2 I interrogate two troubling myths circulating about women and leadership. First, the myths of opportunity suggest that gender equality has been 'won' and that women now compete on equal terms with men in the academic workforce. Second, leadership myths expose populist discourses about women's styles of leadership that perpetuate a particular ideology about what leadership ought to look like and how women leaders in particular ought to behave.

In Chapter 3 I turn attention to women's career patterns and aspirations for leadership. I provide contextual information to offer a backdrop to reading the various narratives. Women who move into leadership roles not only learn how to adapt to the prevailing masculinist culture, they also learn how to strategically manage their positioning as the organizational 'other' as I show. The move into more senior roles is frequently described as accidental (Rose 1998) rather than integral to a personal or professional career strategy. To be successful in these roles, women tactically distance themselves from institutional housekeeping tasks and work to avoid being labelled in particular ways. Accordingly, I highlight ways in which women engage in leadership work that is self-fulfilling and self-affirming.

In Chapter 4 I outline the dynamics and dilemmas women leaders face in the privileged and gendered social order within university management. Through the re-presentation of women's stories, I show the extent to which the leadership game and its gendered rules shape underpinning systems of knowledge, beliefs and practices that dictate the 'fit' with the prevailing institutional culture. Decisions to opt in and play the game, reject the rules, or opt out are seldom straightforward. Women can comply or collude with the rules (Swan and Fox 2010; Thomas and Davies 2002), or reject these rules and be positioned as organizational outsiders (Deem and Ozga 2000). The rules are seldom devised by women and they must learn them in order to survive in academia. Nor do women participate in the game on an equal footing and consequently, from the outset are travellers in a male world.

In Chapter 5 I examine the precarious position that women in senior roles occupy. Due in part to the disproportional representation of women in these positions, women are potentially exposed to extensive criticism and rebuke by their colleagues because they can expose what is missing from an organization. This chapter traverses dangerous terrain as I expose ways in which women leaders do not act in positive and self-affirming ways. Importantly, this chapter looks beyond blaming women as the problem but asks more serious questions about the problem of leadership. However until there is a departure from discourses that normalize male and masculine ways of leading and managing, the complexities of women's lives as leaders cannot be fully understood.

I turn my attention in Chapter 6 to ways in which women seek to change the rules of the leadership game through their work with and on behalf of their female colleagues. Importantly, in this chapter I look at how women make space for themselves as leaders. Mindful of the voices of Indigenous women, I propose alternative models for thinking about 'women' and 'leadership'. My intention is to disrupt narratives about White women's leadership and present a way of thinking about leadership from Indigenous women's perspectives that abandons notions of organizational hierarchy and situates leadership with/in the familial.

In this final chapter I explore possibilities for change. Although the institutional spotlight might concentrate attention on the challenges, contradictions and ambiguities women leaders encounter, the possibility exists that being in the spotlight is a powerful way in which women can bring attention to their leadership strengths and abilities. Women are not powerless. Their power lies in their independence and the uncertainty that their presence creates (Marshall 1984).

Conclusion

This opening chapter provides the contextual background for the book. Specifically I pose the question whether organizational diversity is either possible or permissible in the current managerial climate of higher education. Certainly, the rise of new public management has provided opportunities for some individual women who have seen its pursuit profitable for their careers and salaries. This new and corporatized environment has created unequal working spaces and arrangements as well as uncertainties and inequalities. The marked rise of individual self-interest and hierarchical control and associated regimes of control and accountability has changed what it means to be a leader and undertake leadership work.

This book occupies dangerous terrain. In the first instance, I challenge the recurring view that women share a commitment to a particular leadership style (see here Due Billing and Alvesson 2000; Manning 2002; Sinclair 1998) and that they ought to exercise agency for and on behalf of their female colleagues (Haywood 2005). Second, uncovering the dissonance between how women leaders view themselves and how their female peers perceive them is dangerous as it confronts discourses that suggest women act as mentors, guides and advocates for their female colleagues (Devos 2008; De Vries 2005). Leadership is emotional and messy work. Leadership work is simultaneously dangerous as well as pleasurable. It is dangerous work because it requires agitating for a feminist agenda that can destabilize male colleagues. It is pleasurable work because it involves connecting women through broader networks and alliances both within and across institutions at local and international levels.

One of the constant challenges that universities in particular face is that governments see higher education as a central instrument to boost national efficiency and to cement their role in the global economy. The ability of universities to respond to economic and political change, meet the demands of (competing) public, private and international interests as well as interpret their own trends and performance has had a consequent effect on how universities are governed and managed, as well as public perception of the role and worth of higher education. These changes, as well as the pace of these changes, have had a marked impact on the role and purpose of leaders as well as the perception of how leadership is enacted. But there is still much more to be done to shatter the gendered status quo.

Chapter 2

Troubling myths

In this chapter two central myths about women and leadership are interrogated. Myth one, the myth of opportunity, implies that gender equality has been 'won' and that women now compete on equal terms with men in the academic workforce. The second myth, the leadership myth, exposes populist discourses about women's styles of leadership that perpetuate a particular ideology about what leadership ought to look like and how women leaders in particular ought to behave. In this chapter I also examine the discourses that circulate about women leaders and propose we set aside reductionist views that locate women as the policy 'problem'.

Introduction

Since the 1980s universities in Australia and other nations such as the United Kingdom (UK), Canada, New Zealand and the United States (USA) have undergone rapid and radical changes (Slaughter and Rhoades 2004). The introduction of market-oriented reforms and the restructuring of educational organizations and their workforces were a primary means by which governments could link education more tightly to the economy. 'Best practices' from the corporate sector were imported unproblematically into schools, colleges and universities through the introduction of quality management, audit and inspection regimes, strategic plans, accrual accounting, performance management and close public scrutiny of institutional productivity and performance (Deem *et al.* 2007). The managerialist agenda offered new career opportunities for women eager to ascend the management ladder as they were considered to possess the necessary relational skills to initiate and implement these changes. The language of success accentuated skills and abilities possessed by acquisitive, competitive, entrepreneurial, decisive and authoritative individuals, skills that maintained as dominant certain forms and practices of masculinity (Kerfoot and Knights 1996).

An additional set of pressures has descended on universities that require academics to engage in a new work order that is aligned with increased demands for innovation, internationalization and economic productivity (Marginson 2000). Accordingly, a diverse and mobile workforce within a deregulated market and knowledge society that can cope with and adapt to this changing environment is imperative (Blackmore *et al.* 2010). However, masculinist principles that emphasize quality, productivity and performance have been shown to negatively impact on women (Barry *et al.* 2007). Due in part to these demands as well as unrelenting work pressures, there is little time, energy or space left to debate issues of gender equity, social justice and inclusion. What remains unchanged is the academy as a relentless bastion of male privilege and power (Hansard Society Commission 1990).

Numerous studies across Europe, North America, Australia and New Zealand have documented the struggles and contradictions women in higher education face (Bagilhole and White 2011; Cotterill *et al.* 2007; Fitzgerald and Wilkinson 2010; Morley and Walsh 1996; Salisbury and Riddell 2000; Wyn *et al.* 2000). What emerges from these studies is that men still occupy most of the senior leadership positions. They are the gatekeepers and their rules are not always clear. These rules are supplemented by a set of powerful and troubling myths that highlight the invisible and persistent gendered traditions, regimes and cultures. There are three ways in which the masculinity of work is reinforced. In the first instance, the expectation that work is undertaken on a full-time basis presupposes that there are no external demands such as family and community to be met (Blackwell 2001). Second, the association of management and leadership work with discourses of toughness, stamina and competitiveness, naturalizes the male figure as authoritative (Charles and Davies 2000). Third, characterizations of competition, jealousy and conflict between women (Miner and Longino 1987) create negative judgements about successful women that can produce distance and dissonances between women and work to dissuade women from taking up leadership roles.

Universities thrive on the myth of individualism that reinforces competitive self-interest as well as self-promotion. Entwined in this myth is the notion of merit and the assumption that high-quality work and demonstrated commitment will be recognized and rewarded. Less acknowledged are ways in which the highly masculine culture of the workplace works to discipline and exclude women. The powerful signal sent to aspiring women leaders is that merit alone will not lead to promotion and that securing a senior leadership role is difficult.

Women in male-dominated work environments such as senior university administration are subject to competing demands. On the one hand they are expected to gain respect through acting in feminine ways, yet on the other, they are required to undertake repair work and mediate their own femaleness precisely because they have disrupted the male terrain of management (Connell 2006). Although it may be espoused that women have opportunity for career progression (Cohn 2000), they are frequently confronted with an array of institutional rules that are neither explained nor made explicit (Eagly and Carli 2007; Gherardi and Poggio 2007).

In this chapter I examine two troubling myths circulating about women and leadership. The myths of opportunity suggest that barriers have been removed and that women now compete in the academic workforce on the same terms as their male colleagues (Agocs 2002). Leadership myths suggest women lead in particular ways. The central thesis here is that women possess leadership characteristics that either confine them to roles as institutional housekeepers or limit their potential effectiveness at senior levels.

Myths of opportunity

The introduction of equal opportunity legislation across a number of Western countries in the mid-1970s induced a number of changes in workplaces. In Australia, for example, equal pay legislation was introduced in 1972, the same year that the Equal Employment Opportunity Act was passed in the USA. In a range of other nations, legislation such as the Sex Discrimination Act (1975) in the UK, the Equal Pay Act (1972) in New Zealand and the Equal Treatment Directive (1976) across the European Union signalled the attention to occupational segregation and the intention to address barriers to women's full participation in the workforce. The impact of this changing legislative environment was commented on by Alison (SL):

> In the early days people did not like women leaders because they thought they were too pushy and they put their nose where it shouldn't be and caused upset. I'm not talking about an academic situation although it could be. Because of my connections I was invited by a [government department] to be one of the first ever women to be on a [certain] Board. They chose two female academics ... I went in for my first interview and the Chairman said to me they didn't want any women on the Board. They didn't know me yet. All he knew was that I was a woman and he protested very vigorously [to the government department]. But Government forced it and has pushed for balance on Boards.

Equity legislation and policies emerged from a variety of social movements such as feminism and civil and Indigenous rights. Initially the focus was the identification of the 'lack' of difference and diversity according to race, ethnicity, religion, gender, sexuality and disability. Accompanied by mandatory reporting of equity targets and outcomes, national policies such as equal employment opportunity (EEO) and affirmative action forced a number of changes across the public sector (Bacchi 2004; Jones 2004). This in turn led to the establishment of EEO offices or units, the implementation of a range of EEO training programmes, institutional level policies and targets and changed recruitment, appointment and promotion processes (Blackmore 2009). In addition, parental and family leave, provisions for child care, grievance procedures and leadership and mentoring programmes designed specifically for women have been embedded in workplaces (Agocs 2002; Blackwell 2001).

Legislative changes combined with policies and practices designed to intervene and ameliorate disadvantage have created an enduring assumption that women have secured a level of opportunity and advantage in the workplace. Laudable though these programmes may be, fundamental beliefs that women have primary responsibility to balance home, family and work remain unchallenged. This can render leadership work deeply unattractive and/or a significant struggle. These myths of opportunity suggest that gender equity initiatives have alleviated career barriers for women and that gender gaps have been eliminated (Baker 2012). But there is little recognition in this myth of the burden of family and community responsibilities that women can carry. In Alison's (SL) view:

> [Leadership can] destroy family life and it seems to be even more difficult for women to keep the balance. I think we can see from the political situation that men are very good at keeping the balance. But you know, what is sometimes forgotten, no, usually forgotten, is that men have wives and partners at home. That's where their housework gets done, that's how they get to work long hours. There is invisible help.

Unchanged is the hidden sexual contract of the workplace (Connell 1995) that presupposes that high-status work is a male domain (Fitzgerald 2012b). Within this hidden sexual contract are rules that are neither discussed nor made public. Consequently, women continue to struggle with the constantly changing rules of the academic game. This is well summarized by Sara (academic) as she reflected on the impact of various women leaders she had worked with:

> A second [leader] that I worked with who was female you would probably define as a closet leader [laughs]. She was always in her office and never about engaging in conversations with staff. She had this fixation that everything she did had to be done well. If jobs were dumped on her with a three-second time period to do it she had to drop everything and do it because she had this fixation that it had to be done well. She was very much governed by the demands of people above and I guess by her own personality which required that she do things well to meet the expectations of her manager. Her role as manager of the staff was almost non-existent. At the same time there was another person in the School who manipulated the situation to his own benefit as Anna [Dean] couldn't define roles and tasks below her. He could do that so he then developed his own power base through the vacuum that she produced. It all seemed to be a game.

This example speaks to the performative demands that leaders in general experience (Blackmore 2009) and the dominance of male models of power and authority that women confront. Although Sara offers her perceptions of her female manager, there is a certain level of disdain that this leader 'was always in her office' and that her strategy was to meet all the expectations of her job, even the tasks 'dumped on her'. In order to meet these demands the woman manager appears distracted and accordingly does not confront the male colleague who is developing his 'own power base through the vacuum [that] she produced'. In this example the absence of the female manager created an opportunity for a male colleague to potentially undermine her. It was not the male colleague whose behaviour was scrutinized but the woman manager whose apparent absence in the wider environment was seen as the catalyst for the power game to be played. Sara's observations emphasize the gendered pressures women face (Acker 2012; Due Billing 2011). That is, women are expected to be able to simultaneously manage tasks, people, emotions and challenges to their authority and position.

In an attempt to 'fix' the problem of too few women in senior leadership roles, the solution is frequently touted to be the provision of training or mentoring in the appropriate traits and skills so that women can compete more effectively with men (Devos 2008; Gibson 2006). This solution purportedly minimizes disadvantage through training and the acquisition of skills and knowledge to better assimilate into the organization and become 'one of the boys' who knows the 'rules of the game' (Acker 2010).

It is counterproductive for human resources departments to train women to be more assertive, more decisive and more tough-minded as this is a form of organizational assimilation. This training is a recuperative attempt to assist women to simultaneously manage their 'femaleness' (Wajcman 1998) and to emulate masculine characteristics. Training women to adopt masculinist skills works to reinforce their positioning as the organizational 'other' (Probert 2005), oscillating between feminine and masculine skill sets in order to conform to a predetermined image of leadership (Adler *et al.* 1993; Sinclair 1998). Their female colleagues do not always view women who adopt masculinist ways of working in a positive light. According to Sharon (SL), 'thinking about the notion of stereotypes, women believe they have to act more like men if they are going to be leaders. I have seen patterns like that. It's destructive.' And the view offered from Sara (academic):

> I think there is less acceptance of women in positions of authority from both sexes, sadly. And the force of history, patriarchal history, men have been doing it for so long they are not used to women doing it, so there are some of the problems. And then there will be women negotiating their own lives, that's why child-free women might be better suited to the structures because it is predicated on a male available to work model, that's a liberal model. So women have to negotiate that. It is also what women want out of life and whether they actually want to play the game.

The critical challenge is to confront the terms of the game itself and not simply secure entry for women as legitimate players. Increasing numbers of women in senior positions is only a first-level response that does not necessarily expose prevailing masculinist games. It needs to be accompanied by wider institutional challenges about the nature of the organization and the operation of White male

privilege. Securing entry to senior ranks becomes more about conforming to existing norms rather than challenging structural inequities and institutional cultures.
White women can be equally complicit in the need to create minimal disruption
to the institutional status quo (Blackmore 2010). Typically interventions such as
leadership development programmes focus on their needs as though they coincide
with the needs of all women across the institution. This places additional stress
and burden on Indigenous women and ethnic minority women to fend for themselves. For example Ngaire, an Indigenous woman, expressed her anger that:

> I have yet to work in a place where the needs and aspirations of Māori
> women are front and centre. Somehow we are supposed to know how to
> work in this place, how to survive. Sure, we get to go to training pro-
> grammes. But it's one of those 'one size fits all' models. And then if you
> ask questions, most of the time you are told 'apply this to your own
> context'. What does that mean, my context? How would anyone know
> what my context is especially when most of the time 'my context' [indicates
> with hands] is ignored?

Ngaire's account is indicative of the politics of institutional privilege and exclusion that Indigenous women face. Each encounter with the White institution is
one of continuous struggle and compromise (Aisenberg and Harrington 1988;
Dace 2012). While equity policies and practices oblige organizations to diversify
their workforce and provide the types of training programmes that Ngaire
experienced, essentially the organizational work practices and culture remain
unchanged and unchallenged.

More recently, equity initiatives have been reduced to a set of managerialist
checklists to ensure targets are met and best practice implemented (Morley
2005a). Checklists of progress and equity audits are no less than fabricated artefacts to assure the organization that 'progress' has been made. Past gains have
slowly been eroded as the retreat to individual responsibility and the concomitant prominence placed on values such as self-reliance, efficiency, competition,
merit and individual success produce normative expectations about what it
means to be a successful academic (Fitzgerald and Wilkinson 2010). While
women may have had opportunity to advance in universities, this has not been
cost neutral. There has been a high emotional, physical and intellectual toll as
women have sought to 'work differently. You know, find a space that I can call
my own, find a space where my research is acknowledged and valued' (Judy,
SL). Similarly Sharon (SL) commented that she did not have 'the energy to
think beyond today' as the 'paperwork, the demands, the deadlines, they all get
a bit much' and the net effect of this was that 'I am close to burn out. I am not
sure how much more I can take and the university can expect.'

In the current climate, individuals are extolled to perform in the best interests of the organization (Exworthy and Halford 1999). In terms of institutional
reputation and status, universities value research productivity and the securing

of external competitive grants over any other academic activity such as teaching (Hazelkorn 2011; Marginson 2000). In this competitive environment gendered games continue as individuals work to maximize their own productive worth and self-interest. Academic careers are more likely to be constructed around research productivity and research reputations (Blackmore 2008). Disproportionately women academics are disadvantaged as they invariably carry the higher teaching loads (Lester 2008; Saunderson 2002). Esteem, prestige and productivity in research are hallmarks of a successful academic and what 'counts' in terms of career progression. Equity work simply does not 'count'.

The identification of the 'need' for diversified workforces ostensibly relocates 'diversity' and 'equity' as organizational 'problems' that require a particular set of policies and practices to be brought into play in order to remedy a deficient situation (Bacchi 2004; Carrington and Pratt 2003). The new policy rhetoric is currently about managing diversity that rebounds to the advantage of the organization that can accrue subsequent accolades such as being identified as an Employer of Choice for Women in Australia. Thus, the rhetoric of equity and diversity has a hollow tone when underpinned by the desire for competitive advantage as an employer of 'choice' for women.

Although higher education has responded, albeit slowly, to the policy environment that calls for equality and equity in public educational organizations, noticeably, gender privilege *within* the academy remains. Women are *persistently* and *consistently* underrepresented in leadership positions in higher education, particularly at senior levels. There has been little integration of equity measures into higher education policy due in part to a pervasive (and at times persuasive) assumption that equal opportunities exist (Allan 2008). A universal myth is that the presence of women in the academy is a firm indication that the battle has been won (David and Woodward 1998). However the abysmal numbers of women at senior levels (Morley 2013) does not appear to arouse concerns that the dominance of one group (men) may be a barrier to women's entry. Even though there have been recent increases in women in senior positions in the academy, it will take more than a numerical shift to shatter centuries of gendered traditions, regimes and cultures (Fitzgerald 2012b). Gender equity remains a mirage (Fitzgerald and Wilkinson 2010).

Organizations that seek to 'manage diversity' and then promptly employ women for the purportedly feminine qualities that they bring to their role (Blackmore and Sachs 2000; Haywood 2005) are converting diversity into a new homogeneity of what it means to be a 'woman' and a 'leader/manager'. No attention is paid to the difficulties of holding such contradictory subject positions. As women and as managers their feminine qualities (Coleman 2011) are co-opted around certain roles and responsibilities such as inducting and mentoring new staff, pastoral care of students, arranging social functions and undertaking institutional housekeeping tasks such as committee and compliance work. This work might well be articulated as supporting and enabling organizational change (Gibson 2006). The unambiguous intention is to introduce new regulatory and disciplinary regimes of policy compliance and performance. Women have become the new workers in managerial regimes and an exploitable resource for greedy organizations (Deem 2001).

'Managing diversity', by its very nature and practices, situates women as an organizational resource to be utilized in strategic ways for the benefit of the organization (Itzen and Newman 1995). Market-driven interests in diversity are more about expanding the core business, student numbers, than increasing opportunity and inclusivity (Blackmore and Sachs 2000). Those women who took on roles associated with equity initiatives now face tensions in reconciling equity work with the economic demands of the performative university. Attempts to manage diversity is reductionist as all forms of difference based on class, race, ethnicity, gender, spirituality, socioeconomic background, geographic location, language and ability/disability are collapsed in attempts to provide a 'one size fits all' solution that produces an image of the organization as demographically diverse and culturally inclusive (Battiste 2000; Jones 2004). Unsurprisingly, in a marketized and performative environment, universities have capitalized on diversity and equity not only as a policy driver but also as a way of applauding themselves for the changes that have been made.

Calas and Smircich (1993) contend that while women have 'advanced' into the managerial ranks, all is not what it seems. Women may have infiltrated the male bastion of the university (Hansard Society Commission 1990) but power remains elusive and unevenly dispersed. Arguably any increase in numbers of women creates an intellectual space for women's ideas to flourish and opens up possibilities for different organizational patterns to be created (Morley and Walsh 1996). Gender inequities have not vanished, they are common and mundane and woven into the organizational fabric. How inequity plays out in institutional spaces is illustrated in the comment from Colleen (SL) that:

> The other observation I would make is that in general men who are leaders in this sector seem to be disdainful and preoccupied and selfish. I don't mean selfish in a particularly negative way. I just mean they focus on what they are doing and if it doesn't fit they don't want to know. But women in this sector seems to be overloaded, stressed.... Women are expected help out in a crisis and often buckle under, and there are always crises happening. Men can just cut out and say no: 'I'm going to get this grant in, or I have a book chapter to write', or whatever it is. They have got more clarity. Women seem to me to have role confusion all over the place. Women who operate in that more preoccupied 'I have other priorities way' get judged incredibly harshly.

Joce (SL) provides a further elaboration on this point:

> Taking on some managerial positions in universities means a lot more responsibility. It's like doing the washing up. Somebody has to do it. The

famous thing wives and mothers say is that the men don't care about the state of the house so that's why they do it. I think there is an absolute parallel to this in academic management. I know a lot of women who say I do not want to get into that world. I will work as a lecturer for the rest of my career. They are treated often very contemptuously by the institution, but they just do it. With hindsight, it's hard to know, but I think it would probably have been the smarter way to go: a lot less aggravation.

It is erroneous to conclude that an increase in women managers to some critical mass will inevitably translate into changed organizational priorities and practices. Having more women in positions of power is not a guarantee that changes in culture and attitudes will occur or that women will speak for or work on behalf of their female colleagues. Aroha made this point very clearly:

They [White colleagues] have learned not to ask me for a Māori view. There isn't one, I don't speak for all. But at least Pākehā [White] women know they cannot speak for all women. They get that. How can Pākehā ask me to speak for Māori? How come some of them don't know what this question even means?

Similarly, Hine an Indigenous academic, outlined the specific challenges she faced:

I am not here for me. I am here for *whanau* [family] and that I make a difference for those coming after me. There are expectations around what I will do for *whanau*. It's not about career, it's about giving back, about being around for those who need me to be … I cannot let anyone down.

Whatever immediate advantage women may have obtained as a result of these new opportunities is negated by the double disadvantage of being a woman and a minority (in terms of the statistical picture). Being an Indigenous woman further exacerbates the extra-visibility as well as expectations to work for and on behalf of all peoples of colour (Dace 2012; Fitzgerald 2010).

The image presented by universities to prospective students, industry and the professions and the wider public is one that embraces excellence and innovation, accountability, responsibility and transparency, sustainability and responsiveness, inclusiveness and diversity. It is a moot point whether these institutional discourses match everyday realities.

Discourses and realities

There are three facets to the myths of opportunity that give rise to a particular set of realities. In the first instance, these myths are associated with discourses that suggest that gender equity has been achieved (Leathwood and Read 2009).

Ironically, the introduction and enactment of equality legislation has silenced debates about gender and the unproblematic assumption remains that gender is no longer an issue. The retreat to individual responsibility is inextricably linked with new forms of management that promote individualism, self-reliance, efficiency and mutual obligation and competition in the marketplace. These attributes are presented as gender neutral (Connell 2006) and therefore work to marginalize and exclude women from dominant institutional discourses (Eggins 1997; Keller and Moglen 1987).

In an attempt to highlight the diverse demographic and institutional façades of universities, statistics are frequently quoted that accentuate and celebrate higher enrolment and graduation patterns of female students and increased numbers of women academic staff. This then disproportionately fosters an imaginary that gender is no longer a matter of concern. What these statistics mask is the concentration of women students in the arts, humanities, social sciences and health sciences; all feminized subjects and disciplines that are less prestigious and less likely to attract high salaries on graduation. The logic at work here is that when there are sufficient numbers of women graduates they will enter male-dominated areas and eventually progress up the ladder, thus leading to a more equitable gender composition in the workforce (Baruch and Hall 2004; White 2004). The completion of a doctoral degree, for example, as a pathway into the academy is by no means a guarantee of an academic career. Securing access to academic work is not easy as Wanda (academic) indicates:

> The other thing I have noticed is that the men do not use women sessionals [casual staff]. They use male sessionals. [For a while] I was the only female academic there and I was the only person who had female sessionals. I had men as well, but there were no women employed [by the men] as sessionals. I thought that was fascinating. They have a huge amount of control over [the employment of] sessionals and whether they get to have the runs on the board and can then apply for an academic job.

The second reality of the myths of opportunity is that counting women in is a reductionist view of equity. The myth of numbers rests on a broad statistical picture that fuels suggestions that an ameliorative set of policies and practices will enhance women's access, opportunities and advancement. Interventions such as mentoring programmes, improved promotion policies and processes, clear grievance procedures, flexible work arrangements, access to informal networks and affirmative action programmes are designed to rehabilitate structural problems. What remains problematic is that this myth and the interventions implemented focus primarily on only certain women. That is, White middle-class women who, in much the same ways as their White middle-class male colleagues, continue to reinforce privilege *within* the academy (Acker and Armenti 2004; Blackmore 2010).

Quite simply, the presence of a numerical minority of women has masked the absence of women who have been traditionally marginalized. This is the gendered wedge that continues to operate as a barrier to *full* access and equitable outcomes across numerous race, ethnicity, class and cultural lines. It is frequently Indigenous women and ethnic minority women as well as those who are deemed advantaged by equity policies and practices who are expected to remain vigilant about gender equity policies and practices (Henry and Pringle 1996; Fitzgerald 2010). These are the women who are frequently too tired, overworked or powerless to confront and produce change. Equity legislation and affirmative action practices have principally benefited White middle-class women. What presents as a possibility is for those women in ascending positions of power and influence to work as allies (Dace 2012; Roman and Eyre 1997) to agitate for more widespread dismantling of the imbalances that continue to exist. The quantitative shift in numbers has not been accompanied by sufficient qualitative gender equity that contributes to real change.

The third reality of the myths of opportunity is that new managerialism has contributed to new career advantages for women (Morley 2005a). The reality is that roles linked with quality assurance, pastoral care, student services, human resources and so forth are forms of institutional housekeeping that do little to challenge the hyper-masculinist model of management (Hatcher 2003). There appears to be an institutional expectation that women are 'there for others' and responsible for the emotional wellbeing of colleagues as well as the wider organ-ization. Helen (SL) commented on the pressure that this dual positioning produced:

> I think I am personable and [I] can be democratic, depending on what it is about. I am not always democratic. But you need to bring a lot of people on board with you, but you also need their expertise and input I will be more democratic. But say the University says this has to be done, this is the policy and it has to be implemented, if you are too democratic you can't get anything done. The staff don't really have a say in it. It's being imposed from up on high so basically you have to say this is what the University wants ... but at the end of the day this is what we have to do. So I can be democratic, but sometimes I am not, which is interesting ... because I am a woman people expect me to be really, really consultative and they are shocked. I am not as consultative as some men who I work with and that can be difficult for some people.

Valorizing qualities that have been traditionally marginalized (such as empathy, care and service) merely harnesses the feminine in pursuit of perfor-mativity (Knights and Kerfoot 2004). And it is a shock, as Helen's story indi-cates, when women do not act in predetermined ways. In many ways women are caught between demands for public accountability and collegial expecta-tions about how women ought to lead (McTavish and Miller 2006; Morley and Walsh 1995. Alana's (SL) recollection speaks to this dilemma:

So all my decisions are by committees; they are probably on the large side, but I don't run long meetings because I think they are cruel. My meetings are a max of two hours and we reconvene if they go over two hours … I think I'm the person who got caught with the poisoned chalice. Because people don't want to make these changes and they are now accusing me of top-down management style … this is simply untrue and it's an unpleasant aspect of my job. Since the changes … I have become a compliance monkey.

Both Helen and Alana have found themselves in deeply challenging positions. Both have a clear understanding of how they want to work but are constrained by institutional forces. Accordingly, perceptions of their leadership have been filtered through gendered lenses that position 'men' and 'management' as well as 'women' and 'management' in particular ways (Collinson and Hearn 1996; Schein and Davidson 1993). It has not been their work that has been immediately evaluated but whether they have acted in conventionally feminine ways. Intensely hierarchical institutions such as universities are difficult places for women leaders as they are frequently seen as 'an exploitable resource for new styles of management' (Blackmore 1992: 49). Despite the rhetoric of inclusiveness and diversity, universities do not necessarily provide space and opportunities for women to lead in different ways as Helen's and Alana's stories highlight.

The absence of men in roles linked with softer skills such as staff and student welfare and management, cultural change, relationship building and shorter-term project roles might be because these roles are deeply unattractive to men. That is, women's presence in senior management and administrative roles might be partially explained by the absence of men who have evacuated such tasks to concentrate on their own research, publications and the securing of prestige and status. A further explanation might well be that undertaking institutional housework is required so that male academics are freed from these less important 'domestic' tasks.

Roles, tasks and activities that are predominantly associated with women are seen to be not as prestigious or high status. This work is conceived as 'women's work' and devalued across the organization. Prichard and Deem (1999: 324) have noted that 'the association between the low status and rewards of jobs and the performance of women' is instrumental to the feminization of management that has slowly occurred. The assumption at work here is that increasing the number of women will automatically bring about change (Bown 1999). But until women are in powerful senior positions the feminization of middle management will continue.

Women's capacity for detail and multi-tasking has produced a powerful capability to undertake and 'master' the administrivia that new managerialism demands; compulsive institutional housekeeping. As Acker has contended (1994: 127), 'setting one's own standards for housework ("autonomy") results in compulsive attempts to increase self-worth by repeatedly upgrading performance targets'.

Conversely, when men dominate a field or position numerically, this is coded 'masculine' and accorded a level of status and prestige. Women who do win positions normally assumed to be the domain of senior men (Whitehead and Kerfoot 1998) are subsequently exposed to a backlash as they potentially threaten meritocratic principles. The myths of opportunity carry the suggestion that women gain access to positions based on their gender, not their competence. The ironic reality is that tasks undertaken by women at the middle and senior levels are those that are neither fully completed (such as quality assurance) nor have entirely satisfactory outcomes (such as external audits).

Less known is whether a new barrier has emerged: women competing with *other* women for access to these new management positions that have been created in the restructured university (Metcalfe and Slaughter 2008). Although these new management positions offer an alternative career pathway for women (Morley 2003), an unanticipated consequence is that women are charged with responsibility for auditing and managing targets, performance, and improvements. Quality assurance processes co-opt women into neo-liberal and managerial discourses that run counter to the securing of equitable outcomes.

It is entirely plausible that attention over the past 30 years to equality in employment and the subsequent removal of legal and structural barriers have located women as both the policy 'problem' and the policy solvers. That is, women in middle management positions in universities bear the burden of equity policies and associated performance indicators. Dispersal of responsibility downwards has the net effect of shifting both focus and accountability from the executive (Vice Chancellor [VC]) level and equity policies and practices continue to be located with individual women rather than with men, systems or the state (Bagilhole 2007; Luke 2001). Although there is recognition of the direct correlation between higher productivity and higher levels of gender equity (Probert *et al.* 1998), the shift to individualism, self-reliance, efficiency, mutual obligation and competition that managerialism has demanded over the past two decades has prompted a retreat from the equity agenda. Positioned as the policy problem, women are required to put in place their own solutions and women's 'failure' to move upwards and onwards through the academic hierarchy is a direct result of their own inability to secure senior appointments and promotions. The gendered nature of the universities and leadership in universities remains unchallenged and intact (Currie *et al.* 2002) and myths of opportunity remain in circulation.

Leadership myths

Headlines in management journals, the business press and the wider research literature advocate new kinds of leadership in order for organizations to survive in a complex, ever-changing, and more competitive environment (Kram and McCollom Hampton 2003). These new demands accentuate leadership that encourages ownership of and participation in decision-making, builds networks within and across institutions and offers a flexible and responsive approach to 'client' needs. Leaders are required to demonstrate innovative capabilities, transparency, collaborative approaches to leadership and the ability to multi-task (Deem 2003; Noble and Moore 2006). Leadership traits that are transformational, flexible, collaborative and relationship-oriented (Due Billing and Alvesson 2000; Manning 2002) are assumed to be the domain of women. This perpetuates a popular discourse that there are 'women's styles of leadership'. Less clear is whether these leadership styles help or hinder women's career progression in universities (Doherty and Manfredi 2006).

The management literature portrays leadership as a widely accepted and uncontested 'good' and images of the ideal leader are invariably male and masculine (Sinclair 2004). An interconnected 'problem' is the think-manager-think-male (Collinson and Hearn 1996; Kerfoot and Knights 1996) mantra that automatically positions men as managers and leaders and the 'lack' of being male and masculine as a primary reason for women's inability to secure and undertake senior roles. Second, this problem further presupposes that those women who are successful are either adjunct males who can demonstrate the same level of mastery or transvestite women who masquerade as men (Höpfl and Matilal 2007). Third, any positions that women occupy or work they undertake is rarely defined as leadership. This is what Sinclair (1998) refers to as the invisibility effect whereby women's work is not seen as leadership work but organizational maintenance.

Leadership in universities involves multiple and complex tasks and responsibilities that are, without doubt, physically, intellectually and emotionally demanding. Leadership is exhausting; the bureaucratic demands and institutional pressures are unrelenting, the emotional labour is exacting and the constant call for organizational change and renewal is nothing less than monotonous. As Sinclair (2004) argues, leadership is not simply the act of being a leader, it is the act of leadership that projects 'success' and 'desirable' attributes. Accordingly, the language of leadership extols virtues such as 'commitment', 'energy', 'toughness', 'rational behaviour', 'objectivity' and 'strategic vision'. These are the virtues that women are expected to demonstrate yet men are assumed to 'naturally' possess these skills. Joce (SL) highlighted her own experience:

> The other interesting thing you know was when I went for promotion. I was asked a question which was 'you are very democratic and you get on well with people, can you make hard decisions?' It was really interesting because other people who went through the process weren't asked that. I thought that was really interesting because there were two jobs and the other person who got it was a man who is much more unable to make a decision than me. There was a stereotype because I am a woman and that question had to be asked.

Without doubt, managerial roles have become more time-consuming and more complex. Academic work has been intensified through the implementation of performance agreements, audits, new technologies and demands to increase international prestige. This is echoed by Colleen (SL) who surmised that 'leadership is tough work. It makes you tough, it's tough work.'

There are three prevalent aspects to the leadership myth that have emerged; that women are 'naturally' suited to meeting the demands of the changing workplace, that women exercise leadership in affirming and collaborative ways; and that those who cannot or do not harness the power and patronage of their male colleagues will fail.

Leadership myths suggest that women have moved into middle and senior management positions as a consequence of changing demographic, institutional and professional career patterns. This recent explosion in numbers of women in middle management roles has occurred at a time of intense scrutiny of higher education and the public demonstration of accomplishments in the local and international marketplace. Arguably this has created a bifurcation of academic work between those who manage and those who are managed (Fitzgerald 2012a; Gumport 2000). 'I recall', said Kayla a senior leader, 'that when I started here I was told to ask my line manager if I had any questions. So I was in a line and lined up to be managed.' Similarly Julia (academic) offered her opinion that she found it difficult to 'learn how to manage up. I'd never heard that before I came [here]. This is hierarchy personified.'

Due in part to the introduction of equity and employment legislation, leadership myths reinforce views that women are now 'in the right place at the right time and with the right skills' (Joce, SL). It is not just about being in the right place, it is also about taking on the 'right' roles that are deemed suitable for women: roles ostensibly linked with teaching, administration and service. These are the roles that do not change the academic status quo. Despite these advances into middle and senior management, evidence suggests that once women attain these roles their performance is frequently placed under close scrutiny and that these evaluations are not always positive (Eagly *et al.* 1992).

The second facet of the leadership myth eulogizes what leadership ought to look like and how women leaders in particular ought to behave. These discourses are highly problematic as they rest on universalizing assumptions that all women have similar value positions, that women's leadership is self-affirming and that women exercise leadership in textbook ways (Blackmore and Sachs 2007; Fitzgerald 2010, 2012b). For women to be successful they must conceal and camouflage their female and feminine identities (Eagly *et al.* 1992) as unchallenged authority is generally identified with masculine views of university leadership (Currie *et al.* 2002).

Discourses of women's style of leadership rest on dangerous assumptions. First, these discourses are dangerous because they produce meta-narratives that homogenize 'women' and fail to account for differences between women. These discourses set up expectations that women will care and nurture, control their emotions, be self-sacrificing and display feminine qualities (Acker 2012; Priola 2007) and applied equally to women across race, class, cultural, religious and ethnic lines. Distinctions between women collapse under the weight of these meta-narratives. Second, 'hard' (or masculine) skills such as financial acumen, strategic management, rationality, assertiveness, decisiveness and competitiveness are privileged over the 'soft' and feminine skills that women 'naturally' possess. Women who possess feminine, that is non-masculine, skills and attributes are of value to the organization primarily because they offer the missing elements necessary for organizational improvement (Due Billing and Alvesson 2000). Third, these discourses can idealize the oppressive environment women encounter. That is, the strong woman is one who has overcome oppressive conditions and she is held up as an example that women can succeed. Fourth, these discourses do not question the values embedded in workplaces and the privileging of some forms of work practices over others and no alternative seems possible.

Counterpoints

Sinclair (2004) and Wajcman (1998) have pointed out that moving into management and leadership roles has required women to adopt certain skills, qualities and attributes to enable them to become 'one of the boys' in order to be successful and perform like a man. As Zoe (academic) observed about a woman leader in her previous university:

> I think the negative aspects of her leadership were really not because she was a woman.... The particular person who was a woman was fairly intolerant; very inflexible and pretty insensitive ... I suppose you would say she had a more traditionally masculinist style but she would come out of the room and say 'I'm just so stressed about this. Everyone I am over this.' Our current academic manager would never do that. She might say 'I'm feeling pretty stressed I need some help you know' and that is great. I cannot imagine a man coming out and saying 'I'm just so stressed I can't do it.' It wouldn't happen. But I have never seen another woman act like that.... In a leadership role you don't expect them to behave like that. You expect people on an odd occasion to do something like that but this happened constantly.

But it is not a woman's relational abilities and attributes by which she is judged, but it is her lack of order, logic, direction and rationality that prevents her from being described as successful as the above extract emphasizes. Possessing supposedly feminine skills is either a rejection or absence of hard male skills. Women who do move into leadership roles are rewarded for becoming honorary men yet at the same time are expected to alleviate the absence of 'soft' skills in their male colleagues. Being neither male nor naturally possessing masculine skills inevitably positions women as the deficient 'other'. Sinclair (1998: 74) cautions women to not be:

> seduced by a masculinity which softens itself at the edges, which learns the language of care and consultation but uses this to strengthen the status quo. The danger is that the 'softer' and more feminine skills of leadership may be learned in order to entrench more deeply the subjugation of women and the superiority of a certain kind of masculinity.

There is a counterpoint to this argument. However unappealing the terms 'feminine skills' and 'women's leadership style' might be, they problematize traditional notions of hierarchy, management and leadership. Drawing attention to forms of leadership other than male and masculine does move awareness of gender away from the periphery, however mild the focus. A broad understanding that the de-masculinization of management might enhance organizational effectiveness (Ely *et al.* 2003) offers a strong temptation for more gender inclusive ways of working. Rather than gender-labelling of skills, abilities and attributes, the shift to examining ways of enhancing the qualitative values all leaders possess is a counterpoint to current universalizing discourses.

The price of entry to leadership can be unappealing to women. First, she must abandon her threatening femininity in order to demonstrate that she can comply with male expectations that she exercise strong and authoritative leadership. It is not simply a case that she become an honorary man, but that she reject the feminine. Ironically this further implies a degree of impotence on her part; women cannot be men, they can only masquerade as men. She is always the deficient 'other' who is expected to 'be good' rather than 'do good' (Blackmore and Sachs 2007). Second, her entrance to leadership exposes the characteristics lacking in the organization – sensitivity, collegiality, emotional management and so on. Organizations spend considerable amounts of money employing consultants and trainers to develop the people skills of their mostly male managers – in other words, training that encourages men to behave like women. That men apparently 'lack' these skills becomes a matter of organizational concern, that women possess these skills is seen as deficiencies that need to be corrected. To be successful women have to compensate for being female by adopting male characteristics. But women can unsettle the benchmark men through their questioning of the status quo and insistence on alternative strategies, priorities and values.

Women wanting to advance to senior leadership roles are evaluated against benchmarks set for and by their male peers. And it is these benchmark men who promote token women to senior positions. As Bagilhole (2000: 9) explains:

> Even if a 'token' woman is allowed to enter the pipelines of power, they are actively discouraged in recruiting more 'like them' or from competing with men for the very top positions. In this way, men maintain their values and

ideas as the dominant ones and ensure the continued success of people as similar as possible to themselves.

The presence of token women works to assure the organization that gender equity has been achieved and leaves intact the masculinist institutional culture and values. For as long as the status quo remains unchallenged, the stark absence of numbers of women in senior leadership roles will continue. Yet the very presence of women in these positions is appropriated by universities in annual reports, employment advertisements, on websites and in glossy marketing materials as evidence of an institutional commitment to gender equality. Kathleen (SL) offered a cogent reminder of the chilly climate women face:

> It's an interesting thing for me because as I said I've been a professor for 17 or so years, and when I first became a professor I was the sole female on every committee. I was just wheeled out so much, and I got totally overwhelmed and thought I've just got to go back to being an associate professor. This is terrible, you know, I don't seem to do anything except go to meetings. I need to be less available and give myself some space.

Those women who do succeed are often expected to do much of the emotional management work of the organization in what is seen as a 'natural extension' of their traditional and domesticated labour. Such work is part of the invisible, traditionally feminized labour of organizations in which 'soft' people skills are viewed as making women, and some men, naturally good at the relational aspects of management while simultaneously locating them in the role of change agents (Blackmore and Sachs 2007). The softening of some forms of masculine management through the rhetoric of care may in fact 'entrench more deeply the subjugation of women and the superiority of a certain kind of masculinity' (Sinclair 1998: 74). The entrée of women into management does not signal that significant shifts in culture or in organizational power relations have occurred.

Leading and leadership are calibrated against targets set through institutional plans and performance agreements. For women this means their performance is subject to expectations set by their male colleagues; the benchmark men who determine what counts as success. Measurement against the standards and norms set by men immediately works to disadvantage women (Mavin 2006; Wilson 2005). Continually judged because of their gender, women in university management have very different experiences of the role and their outsider status that is further exacerbated across race, ethnicity and class lines (Corsun and Costen 2001; Dace 2012; Rhode 2003). Alternatively, some women's 'outsider' status may offer them a form of positive capital as universities seek to commodify the cachet of women's diversity from an assumed White, masculinist leadership norm (Blackmore 2010; Fitzgerald and Wilkinson 2010).

Conclusion

Competing demands to be globally productive have provoked the resurgence of conservative ideologies (Allan 2008) that emphasize choice, diversity, markets, standards, equity and strong leadership. These ideologies have further prompted wider reform across the public sector to reduce expenditure, increase outputs, benchmark performance and introduce private sector models of management (Clarke and Newman 1997). Although universities have responded rapidly to the demands of new managerialism and market imperatives, support for gender equity has been slow.

Historically studies have shown that men have dominated senior positions in the academy (Bailyn 2003; Brooks and Mackinnon 2001; Morley 1999), that equity has been difficult to secure (Fitzgerald and Wilkinson 2010) and the gender pay gap remains (Baker 2012). In other words, the picture has not changed. Women who do reach senior levels confront issues that all leaders in complex bureaucracies face, but they confront quite unique issues in their challenge to the status quo (Eggins 1997).

Women who do venture into the predominantly male territory of senior management are indeed 'travellers in a male world' (Wajcman 1998: 50); a world in which the climate is inhospitable and women are viewed as outsiders (Bagilhole and White 2008; Glazer-Raymo 1999) primarily because they do not belong. As outsiders in the sacred grove (Aisenberg and Harrington 1988) women feel the need to prove themselves able to accomplish the task and to meet expectations of their colleagues. This is further complicated as some women find themselves in the 'velvet ghettos' of communication, finance and human resource management (Guillaume and Pochic 2009), or languishing in what was described by the late Joan Eveline as the 'ivory basement' (2004).

Any anticipation of change that equal opportunites, affirmative action and equity policies may have signalled is dwindling. And while it may sound like a tired and rehearsed argument, intransigent barriers that serve to alleviate inequities seriously undermine any organizational culture, norms and practices. Institutionalized gendered structures and cultures may not have the capacity to respond to contemporary challenges. Significantly, the shifting landscape of higher education and the increasing emphasis on collaborative ways of working, new technologies, demands for high productivity and performance, as well as the impact of local and international benchmarking exercises arguably call for new forms of leadership as well as leaders who are able to respond to the demands of new managerialism.

Chapter 3

Patterns and pathways

In this chapter I turn attention to women's career patterns and aspirations for leadership. I provide contextual information to offer a backdrop to reading the various narratives. Women who move into leadership roles not only learn how to adapt to the prevailing masculinist culture, they learn how to strategically manage their positioning as the organizational 'other' as I show in this chapter. The move into more senior roles is frequently described as accidental (Rose 1998) rather than integral to a personal or professional career strategy. To be successful in these roles, women tactically distance themselves from institutional housekeeping tasks and work to avoid being labelled in particular ways.

Introduction

The academy conjures up images of a community of scholars and public intellectuals with a high degree of academic autonomy and professional discretion, a high commitment to collegiality, consensus decision-making and professional critique through peer review. There is an institutionalized intellectual hierarchy that has historically been the bastion of male academics and which has afforded limited access and advancement to women academics (Brooks and Mackinnon 2001; Fitzgerald 2009; Morley 1999). Women who venture into senior management can feel like intruders (McIntosh 1985) because they are not always immediately welcomed. But what this evokes is the image of women as the organizational 'other'; they are different from men as well as from their women colleagues.

Traditionally conceptualizations of academic leadership were linked to professorial authority derived from teaching, research and scholarship. The promise of the reform agenda was that opportunities in new organizational structures would be available (Allan 2008; Clarke and Newman 1993). Unanticipated was the increase in executive power and the alignment of universities with corporate modes of governance and management (Blackmore *et al.* 2010; Bradley 1999). The pre-reform imagined community of collegiality and reciprocity was in direct contrast to the post-reform public image of accountability and relevance (Deem *et al.* 2007; Slaughter and Rhoades 2004).

Management has increasingly become conflated into leadership and, while power has been distributed upwards, much of the responsibility has been dispersed downwards. Key policy and resource decisions as well as strategic directions are retained at the executive level and cascaded down through the organization through the management hierarchy (Deem 2004; Exworthy and Halford 1999). Leadership roles in universities are now strongly linked to job descriptions, budgets, strategic plans and performance targets (Fitzgerald 2012a). In order then to meet the demands of the modernized university, there is an unspoken assumption that this work is conducted full time and in flexible ways. This flexibility rebounds to the benefit of the organization as pressures for productivity, compliance and accountability increase (Bryson 2004; Durbin and Tomlinson 2010). At the corporate heart of the organization, leaders must not only self-manage and self-regulate, they must now induce their staff to perform in similar ways.

The overt level of performativity that is embedded in the senior management roles, the intense time commitment, the high level of institutional visibility, as well as expectations that women will undertake a gendered chain of care are integral to the career experiences of women leaders (Acker 2012). This may involve care for the staff and/or care for the institution. The immediate challenge women face is that they are expected to take up this care work: work that reinforces the institutional status quo (Gherardi and Poggio 2007) and which does not necessarily advance women's careers (Perriton 2006). For example, Lindsay, a senior lecturer, thought her dean 'saw herself as saving lost souls' and that 'she fights to save them' as 'they are not academically strong, not getting the research outputs'. In complicated ways this dean was simultaneously involved in the care of staff and care of the organization so that targets were met. The staff member's overall performance was of concern to the dean as any deficiency would reflect poorly on her. Lindsay's recollection is bordering on the evangelical with mention of 'lost souls' and 'fights' to 'save' a staff member.

Restructuring in universities has produced a sharp divide between those who manage and those who are managed (Davidson and Burke 2000; Deem 2003). Similarly, the focus on financial targets and fiscal efficiency has prompted a downsizing of permanent or continuing staff, amalgamations across university faculties and schools, redeployment of staff from areas of least student demand to subjects and disciplines with greater numbers and the casualization of the academic workforce (Bryson 2004; Kimber 2003). Evident in numerous universities is a flexible, peripheralized and feminized workforce whose primary tasks centre on teaching, assessment and pastoral care routines (Acker and Feuerverger 1997). The academic environment is now marked by performance assessments and research audits that recognize and reward compliance with man/agerial imperatives (Collinson and Hearn 1996). The emphasis has shifted from intrinsic scholarly rewards to measurable outcomes in terms of research outputs, research grants, income generation from consultancies for which the institution derives prestige and status (Hazelkorn 2011; Marginson 2000).

In this environment strong emphasis is placed on entrepreneurial management and individual competitiveness (Miner and Longino 1987). Management is projected as an objectively defined set of capabilities and rational dispositions that are discharged by those in positions of authority and power (Deem 2003). Effective senior management requires a relentless commitment to the organization both in work and out of formal work hours.

Women who move into leadership are no longer a rare presence in the academy, yet they remain exceptional as university senior management remains conventional male terrain. Consequently womens' stories are punctuated with the challenges they face and their positioning as the organizational 'other'; they are cast as other to their female colleagues who remain in the lower rungs of the academic hierarchy and other from those considered 'natural' inhabitants of the ivory tower (Eveline and Booth 2004; Fitzgerald 2012b). Despite the myriad challenges (Haywood 2005; Lester 2008), women do actively seek leadership roles, however bleak the statistics.

The illusion of inclusion

Speaking to the National Press Club in Canberra (Australia) to mark International Women's Day in 2011, Minister for the Status of Women, the Honourable Kate Ellis noted that 'there is a dearth of women in leadership positions in this country and it is in the best interests of our nation economically to ensure that these trends are reversed' and that a Workplace Gender Equality Agency would have greater powers to 'drive gender equality in Australian workplaces' (Ellis 2011). Worryingly, the emphasis on individualism, self-reliance, efficiency, accountability and competition in modernized organizations has provoked a retreat away from the equity agenda. The hope for a changed future that equal employment opportunities, affirmative action and equity policies promised is diminishing.

Although women now comprise the majority of students in many countries (Leathwood and Read 2009), and more women are moving into middle and senior level positions in universities (Bagilhole and White 2011), there is a precarious gender imbalance in senior leadership and management roles (Clegg and McAuley 2005; Fitzgerald 2012a; Morley 2005b). Once women are at these senior levels, they then encounter the power of male hegemony that can accommodate the presence of some women, but has little or no tolerance with having its dominance challenged (Benschop and Brouns 2003; Blackmore and Sachs 2007; White 2001). The internal demographics do little to assure even the casual observer that universities are equitable places. This is the illusion of inclusion that runs counter to the realities of exclusion that dominate academia.

Despite optimism that the feminization of the paid workforce in the twentieth century, the introduction of gender equity policies, affirmative action practices and equal employment legislation would bring about profound changes

(Blackmore and Sachs 2000; Probert 2005), challenges and negotiations remain for women in higher education (Cotterill *et al.* 2007). Although women have gradually encroached on the previously almost exclusive world of senior management in higher education, their presence remains a statistical minority.

White *et al.* (2011) report that in the 39 public Australian universities women comprise 40 per cent of the pro vice chancellors (PVCs), 34 per cent of deputy vice chancellors (DVCs), yet only 18 per cent of vice chancellors (VCs), were women. In South Africa 17 per cent of women are VCs and in Portugal only 7 per cent of VCs are women. At present only 13 per cent of leaders in higher education institutions in Europe are women, and 9 per cent of research-intensive universities have a female head (Enders and de Weert 2009; Sagaria 2007). At the forefront of these statistics is Sweden where in 2010 the proportion of women in senior positions reflects sustained attention to gender equity policies. As documented by Peterson (2011: 621), in Sweden 43 per cent of VCs, 60 per cent of DVCs and 31 per cent of deans are women. Iceland, Norway, Finland and Israel also have high numbers of female rectors (VCs) while in Denmark, Cyprus, Lithuania, Luxembourg and Hungary there are no women VCs (Morley 2013).

In Ireland the situation is particularly bleak. Men occupy 85 per cent of the management roles, men are eight times more likely to be in positions at the level of dean and above and five times more likely than their female colleagues to be promoted to the professorial level (O'Connor 2008). At the time of writing, of the elite 24 Russell Group of universities in the UK, currently only the University of Manchester (Professor Dame Nancy Rothwell) and London School of Economics and Political Science (Professor Judith Rees) have women VCs. Breakwell and Tytherleigh (2008) have found that in Britain VCs were likely to be white, male and with an average age of 57.76 years and typically had either undergraduate or postgraduate degrees from Oxford or Cambridge Universities. In the United States, four of the eight Ivy League universities have had women presidents: Ruth J Simmons at Brown in 2001, the first Black leader of any Ivy League institution, Drew Gilpin Faust at Harvard (2007), Shirley M Tilghman at Princeton (2001), Judith Rodin at the University of Pennsylvania in 1994 whose successor was Amy Gutmann in 2004. Notable that these achievements are, across the 800-year history of universities, the exclusion of women has been a marked historical reality.

Ultimately men in high-status subjects or disciplines and from high-status universities secure roles as vice chancellors (Morley 2013). For example, Bagilhole and White (2008) identified that the majority of VCs in the UK and Australia originated from science, engineering and technology backgrounds. It is on this academic assembly line that different career patterns and choices can be made (Barry *et al.* 2001).

In March 2008 the only woman VC to head a New Zealand university across its 139-year history resigned. At the time of writing there are no women VCs in any one of the eight universities in New Zealand. This is particularly appalling given that this is a nation known for its historical socially inclusive policies and legislation (Fitzgerald 2009). Although statistics across a range of nation-states show that numbers of women at the senior levels have increased, ratios remain abysmal. In addition, women tend to be clustered in disciplines such as Education, Health and Social Work (Ducklin and Ozga 2007; Fitzgerald and Wilkinson 2010). A numerical increase does not necessarily shatter the exclusionist culture of higher education or act as a catalyst for radical transformations of traditional organizational patterns.

For Indigenous women the academy can be an intensely lonely and colonizing place. Their White women colleagues are scarce in numbers but they are usually not the sole woman at senior levels and will have colleagues across institutions from whom they can garner support. Statistics for Indigenous, migrant, ethnic minority and women of colour are woeful. The 2011–2012 Higher Education Statistics in the UK, for example, show that while one in five, or 20.5 per cent of professors are women, women comprise 47.3 per cent of the non-professorial workforce. An even bleaker pattern reveals that one in 13, or 7.7 per cent of professors are Black and Ethnic Minority (BME) women, and BME women are in 13.2 per cent of other academic posts (Higher Education Statistics Agency 2013). Indigenous women confront two dominant cultures in the academy; male and White.

Given their numerical dominance in less senior roles (such as associate lecturer and lecturer), women find themselves with workloads that have high teaching or administrative components that in turn directly impact on research agendas and activities. A recent survey of higher and further education in Scotland found that women spend greater proportions of their time than men on teaching and related administrative duties (McTavish and Miller 2007). Hence, it is not surprising that an analysis of the high-stakes Research Assessment Exercise (RAE) in the UK (known as the REF or Research Excellence Framework from 2014 onwards), and the emphasis on research outputs as a key criterion for career advancement showed that only 32 per cent of women academics were likely to be counted as research active compared with 52 per cent of male academics (Association of University Teachers 2004). Similarly Morley (2005a) reported that in the 2001 RAE, fewer than 25 per cent of panel members and one in seven chairs were women and that those panels chaired by women were responsible for allocating less than 10 per cent of the RAE funding. But it is not simply that women teach more and research less. Both men and women are experiencing high workloads (Bryson 2004) but the gender difference lies in the significant informal emotional management work that women undertake.

Pressures and performance

The renewed focus on targets, measurement, cost centres and cost drivers, performance management, standards and productivity dominate management work in universities (Deem 2001; Gumport 2000; May 2005). Position descriptions privilege the functional, financial and strategic over the interpersonal and educational aspects of leadership roles. Being a manager and doing management is more about policy, performance and productivity than people. The organizational message is about control, competition and conquest. A comment offered by Sheryl (SL) accentuated the impact of these changes:

> The work here is relentless. Bureaucracy and paper work. That about sums it up. I have to fill in columns on spreadsheets about the budget, about staff research, about teaching scores. I now have spreadsheets for staff workload calculations. And then I find out everything is going on line. So I dutifully fill it out online too and then the system falls over. So it's back to the paper trail to count what I do, what the staff do. I have to be able to reduce it all, reduce staff to a column on a spreadsheet.

At the core of these new work forms is individualized entrepreneurialism (Bryson 2004; Slaughter and Rhoades 2004) and competitive individualism. Academics are required to be self-sufficient and market-oriented individuals in relentless pursuit of prestige, esteem and career advantage (Blackmore 2009). There is no clear end to the amount of time required to undertake this work. Institutions have become greedy in terms of the levels of commitment, work productivity and emotional engagement expected of staff (Butterwick and Dawson 2005; Currie *et al.* 2002). Academic career structures increasingly demand single-minded attention to developing a high level of scholarly expertise, increasing research productivity and building international esteem.

The career portrait of the twenty-first-century academic is one who travels regularly, has worked and resided in several countries, may have held appointments in several institutions, is competitive and results-oriented, has extensive networks, undertakes international consultancies and is able to cope with increasing demands to produce research that meets institutional and national priorities (Fitzgerald *et al.* 2012). The successful career academic is more likely to be in the fields of science, technology or engineering; all fields dominated by men (McTavish and Miller 2009).

Informal skills and expertise that women as campus citizens bring to their roles do not accrue the same levels of esteem and prestige (Park 1996). The emotional labours of academic life do not easily or readily find a place on an academic CV (Miller and Morgan 1993). For example, Joan (academic) offered her view that:

> I am not sure I will ever move into a leadership role. Sure, being a professor is a goal. But I look now at women across the university. The hours, the pressure ... and most of them look exhausted most of the time.

Another academic woman, Debra made the point that:

> getting a name for yourself in academia is about research and research dollars. It's the grants, the pubs [publications] and the invitations. That's

the game for me. Reality check here. Leadership work is one line on my CV. Publications, well that can take as many lines as I want it to. That's the lines on the CV anyone is ever interested in.

Collegial research networks are crucial as they act as a means of transmitting, reproducing and reinforcing academic norms and expectations as well as a means of socialization into the scholarly profession. Those who are excluded cannot acquire knowledge about which journals and publishers are prestigious, how research projects are judged and funded, which individuals to meet at conferences, how to garner invitations to scholarly networks and which individuals to nominate as referees on employment and promotion applications. Promotion then becomes more difficult to secure because research productivity is a non-negotiable aspect of academic work and career advancement (Bain and Cummings 2000) and the institutional maintenance roles that women predominantly undertake do not accrue the same levels of recognition and prestige.

Winning research bids, publication and participation in research audits (Hazelkorn 2011) as well as access to eminent senior scholars as mentors are the critical indicators of academic success. In the current environment in which universities seek to publicly demonstrate their relevance and the worth of staff, the internationalization of research work is an organizational imperative. This includes securing funds from international sources, international research collaborations, and international esteem such as visiting professorships. These are the activities that receive the highest rewards in terms of status, promotion, esteem and recognition. It is the combination of these factors that then leads to financial rewards accumulated through salary increments, promotion or market allowances (Blackmore 2008). Having the flexibility to undertake these activities and the careful manufacture of one's esteem and prestige ultimately adds 'value' to the individual and the organization.

The academic career legend suggests then a trajectory that is uninterrupted, rational and linear and marked by stages of achievement and the accrual of experiences and measurable outputs. This leads to women being generally less than successful in applying for promotion as their career trajectory is uneven (Carrington and Pratt 2003) and interruptions to career for the bearing, caring and raising of children may not be fully taken into account. Being a mother as well as being a productive academic is highly challenging as Grummell et al. (2009: 192) point out:

> The highly individualized capitalist-inspired entrepreneurialism that is at the heart of the academy has allowed old masculinities to remake themselves and maintain hegemonic male advantage.... As women are significantly less likely to be care-free than men, regardless of their age or status, their capabilities for satisfying performative demands are lesser within the new managerial regime.

Within the promotions process itself, the emphasis on selection criteria such as merit, status and prestige (Bagilhole and Goode 2001; Fitzgerald 2012b) contributes to a gendered view of academic work and academic worth. In particular, as emotional management work cannot be quantified or evidence necessarily produced, these contributions are frequently overlooked. Bonnie, an academic, recalled her experiences:

> I'm on the mommy track. Are you not familiar with that phrase? It's an American phrase. They normally call it the mommy track. It basically implies that because you have children it's the opposite of the fast track. You go home at 5 p.m., this is in corporate places; you don't travel much; you don't go that extra mile; you get to do jobs like looking after students because you're around all the time.

Combining academic work and motherhood (Raddon 2002), in Jacqueline's (academic) opinion, had been costly in terms of her own career trajectory:

> I was promoted to senior lecturer. But I had also made the decision to take some time away and have a child. My research effort was zilch in those years. Now I have caught up with myself a bit. After being knocked back for promotion last year I decided that I would never again apply for promotion until I am so ready it is ridiculous.

This is not an unusual example as women constantly report waiting until they are certain to be promoted before they will apply (Acker 1994). Tenure and promotions processes that require individuals to demonstrate how their performance has been aligned with and contributed to organizational goals do not necessarily account for career breaks (Rose 1998). Although promotion policies and processes may take into account varying career patterns (Probert 2005), academic work is performed in an organizational climate that is predominantly associated with the masculine subject (Hey and Bradford 2004; Gherardi and Poggio 2007). Any move into management is not particularly smooth for women as they are deliberately straying on to male territory.

Moving into leadership

The numerical dominance of women in the lower rungs of the academic hierarchy inevitably connects women's academic work with teaching and student services and the majority of men with research, publications and academic prestige (Leathwood and Read 2009; Noble and Moore 2006). Those women who hold senior positions in universities are more likely to be enagaged in work centred on organizational development and institutional change (Deem et al. 2007; Morley 2003). The more senior the position in a university, the more likely it is to be associated with management roles. It is the norm in most universities across Australia, New

Zealand, Canada and the UK that professorial staff act as head/chair of the school/department for a period of time and then return to her/his substantive position. University administration and leadership as a career path ostensibly is a move away from the core of academic work; teaching and research (Lafferty and Fleming 2000). As one woman participant remarked:

> What makes academic leadership very problematic is that you don't come into the university to do administrative roles: that's the problem. You come in because you want to teach or you come in because you want to research and the leadership roles are inflicted on us, that's the problem. It used to be that people would apply for the job and that's what they knew they would be doing. That's not the case now. What happens now is that you know you have people who have worked their way up and may have performed very well ... but just because you do something well doesn't mean you are going to do everything well and be a great leader, and that's what has happened. I think that's really problematic and really one of the reasons why some women are not wanting to take on higher leadership roles. I didn't come in to do that. I am not good at it. I don't see it as strength and yet I feel quite guilty saying that.

Similarly, Louise and Christine (see below) indicated that leadership roles had not been their preferred career track and both felt that they had no choice but to serve a time as head of their respective schools:

> I knew it was my time. I couldn't avoid it [head of school] really. It was a five-year term and I knew that my research would take a huge hit. I was consumed by management and university demands. And when it all finished I remember feeling that I was left with nothing other than a line on my CV. I'd done no research for five years and so had no grants under way and no publications. It would take me about two years to get back on track. So the job really cost me seven years. It felt liked I had stopped being an academic the minute I became a manager.
>
> (Louise)

> I didn't want to be one of those professors who did everything. You know, manage the department, do research and teaching, and turn up to all the meetings. I just couldn't spread myself around like that. I knew it was for a short period of time I had to do admin but staring down three years it seems like a lot longer. Why does this university do this to us? I knew being a prof[essor] meant time away from academic work. I was promoted because of my research, my teaching, and then I got to do something that was not about this. So I got to be a prof and then the next thing I knew I got to be a Head of School.
>
> (Christine)

Both women identify with being an academic and struggle with the move into management. For both their term as head of school was relatively short as this middle management role is usually of limited tenure (between two and five years). Louise and Christine were conscious that their work as academics stalled once they took on management roles and make the point that there was a high cost to this revolving form of management. Louise, for example, estimated it was a seven-year term away from being a productive academic and Christine admitted she was unprepared to take on this role as a newly appointed professor. Being in a management position required both women to separate their identities as academics and managers (Deem 2003; Gini 2001). Moving into management was viewed as a lose/lose situation. There was as sense of loss of self as an academic as well as a loss of self in becoming a manager. What their stories indicate is that both were confident about their identity as academics but as both were unaware of the expectations and possibilities of leadership, this caused a level of anxiety and uncertainty. In many ways, being an academic and being a manager were 'two deeply structured and mutually exclusive' roles (Bascia and Young 2001: 278).

Although both women viewed middle management as 'time away from academic work' (Christine) and that they had 'stopped being an academic' (Louise), at the end of their term both decided to move to more senior roles. 'I thought it wasn't for me', mused Christine, 'but I got to like being at the big boys' table, knowing what was going on, being part of the decision-making. So here I am. A bit of an accidental turn into management really.' Louise similarly remarked that 'I did not think I'd like it [management]. But I wanted to do a good job and then the more I got into it, the more I realized I could make a difference about the place.' Thus, being exposed to the dispositions of the job and learning 'how things work' (Louise) prompted both women to seek more senior roles. While neither had aspired to leadership roles, this unplanned period as middle managers created new, if not accidental, career opportunities. In one instance, Christine's participation 'at the big boys' table' had stimulated her decision to apply for a more senior role. Perhaps serendipitously, toward the conclusion of their middle management terms senior management positions were advertised at each of their respective institutions. Both were motivated to apply and both were successful. However, as Wajcman (1998) notes, any reluctance on their part to apply for this senior position might have been seen as a lack of commitment or a lack of ambition.

Karen (SL) had to prove that she could do the job before she was formally appointed:

> I'd effectively been doing the job for years. Everyone knew that XX was hopeless and relied on women to do their jobs as well as his. I applied for his job. I got interviewed and then told that no appointment would be made. I then got offered the job for six months. Then one Friday, I was asked to see the VC and he offered me the job. He said something to me

like 'you've shown you can do the job, that's all I need to know'. I think I was supposed to be flattered.

In this situation Karen was an apprentice for six months in order to prove that she could do the job. There had been no recognition of her previous work in this role when she had originally applied and she was of the belief that 'they were trying me out. See if I was like them.' Being 'like them' placed Karen under a great deal of surveillance to ensure that she could 'do the job'. As she was the first woman appointed to this role, the legacy of her male predecessors hung over her head. 'It took me quite some time', she continued, 'to have the maintenance department carry out the request to remove XX's portrait from my office' and that it was only when 'I was seen carrying a hammer that there seemed to be any action'.

Motivations to move into senior management roles were varied. Many women made career choices based on financial reasons, or sought positions in different geographical locations because their partner had relocated or adult children had established their own homes there. Some remained at one university for most of their career because they were particularly committed to the organizational priorities (David and Woodward 1998; Davidson and Burke 2000). In the main, women's career trajectories into management were informed by their professional *and* personal circumstances; fitting in with family or fitting in with the organization.

A further aspect of the accidental move into management was that many women acted in roles for a period of time and either derived pleasure from this new work or did not see the job as unattainable. Kathleen, for example, was not deterred from applying for a senior role because 'I had been acting in the role and that helped me to decipher the PD [position description]. I knew I had done a good job too and I wanted to continue.' The security of knowing that they possessed the requisite skills, knowledge and abilities prompted a number of women to apply for senior roles. As Melissa (SL) noted:

> Acting as Dean for a period of time was a career break for me. I came to realize I could do the job and that I wanted this kind of career move. I had thought about it before but I did not have that line on my CV. You know 'Acting Dean'. Until I had that time as Dean I would not have been a serious contender. I can now say I have done this and done that. I have looked around and I know what happens. Jobs are advertised but it is usually a current Dean wanting to move institution that seems to get the job. It's hard to break into that level if you haven't been there before. I also thought about myself as a Dean so I thought – why not?

Melissa was able to present herself as a dean as a 'line on my CV' as well as draw on her experiences while acting in a position (a period of 12 months) in order to put herself forward as a candidate.

Moving into a formal leadership position required a number of personal and professional changes. Alice (SL) explained this as 'management means you have to establish boundaries and as much as you want to, you just can't go back. You just have to move away from it all. I'm still friendly with colleagues, but I am not their friend.' Here Alice was caught between her personal friendships and attachments and having to identify as a manager and 'move away from it all'. Initially her colleagues struggled to understand what had occurred. As Megan (academic) recalled, 'We were all shocked when Alice moved to that role. Shocked because she seemed to have nothing more to do with us. She had other people around her all the time.' Alice was caught between her previous role as a head of school and her colleagues' perceptions and the need to re-present herself in a new role. Alice had to accommodate the new practices and priorities expected of her PVC portfolio and in doing so peripheralized her colleagues.

Career advancement for Alice was associated with a degree of personal loss of friendships and a new level of awareness of her own position in a larger institution (Avis 2002). She was required both to perform (leadership) as well as to provide evidence that she was performing successfully by establishing new networks and new collaborations (Coleman 2011; Sinclair 2004). In this example it was important to Alice to separate her new positional authority from her previous role. What occurred was that Alice had 'move[d] away' in order to emphasize the distance between her former and new role. A certain level of toughness in rejecting her former role and showing solidarity to her new (senior) networks was necessary for Alice to be perceived as competent (Wagner and Wodak 2006; Fletcher 2004).

Many of the participants described ways in which their gender created opportunities to move into management roles (Chesterman and Ross-Smith 2006). For example Rachel (SL) stated that she thought:

> I knew when I applied for the job that there weren't any women at this level in the university. So I figured out that there was some kind of pressure on the VC to appoint women. The Chancellor was a woman and she had made all sorts of statements about the need to change the gender balance. The university also wanted to maintain its status as an Employer of Choice for Women and so the pressure was on. My track record certainly got me to the interview.... But I have spent most of my time trying to get other women in the door. I'm not sure the VC gets that equity means employing more than one.

In this instance gender provided Rachel with limited situational advantage as the VC was mindful of the dearth of women in senior roles. However, the net result was that Rachel was the sole woman on the senior management team. The inclusion of one woman on the senior management team appeared to be the solution and the masculinist policies and practices of the university remained intact. Here again Rachel was well aware of the challenges she faced. 'In many ways,' she said, 'I was the token woman. Or at least that's what they thought. But I sure didn't act like that. I made myself known. I spoke up and spoke out about matters that concerned me.'

The seduction of management as well as opportunities to work in different ways and to make a difference were powerful drivers in women's decisions to move to more senior roles. 'I knew I could do it,' Lynette said, 'and I'd acted in the role. I hated the pressure but I loved being able to make change happen.' Positioned in a highly visible and powerful role, working in a fast-paced environment, being able to make proactive decisions and provide immediate solutions gave women an intense feeling of satisfaction about their work. For example, Cecilia (SL) outlined the factors in her decision to apply for her current job:

> You know, I didn't think management was for me. The hours, the stress and the pressure. But after a few years I thought, yeah I can do this, I'm good at this. It is still stressful but I get to see the impact of decisions I've made and how the place is now better, much better than it used to be. It's satisfying really.

Hidden behind this narrative are the struggles and compromises that Cecilia made in order to 'fit in' and 'show I can cope'. Cecilia admits that it took her 'some time' to 'organize work' as well as 'organize life, you know, the house, the kids, myself'.

Balancing acts

While new managerialism proffered the impression that it was gender-neutral primarily because opportunities for women were created through meritocratic performance, the reality was that traditional hierarchies were redrawn. The resulting cultural and leadership patterns privileged the masculine in terms of management and organizational values and practices and excluded or constrained femininity (Goode and Bagilhole 1998). The highly individualized and entrepreneurial focus of modern universities (Slaughter and Rhoades 2004) maintains hegemonic male advantage. In this competitive environment, the ideal worker continues to be seen as one with no interests or responsibilities outside of work (Bagilhole 2000; Bailyn 2003; Probert 2005; Siemieńska and Zimmer 2007). As women are significantly less likely than men to be care-free (David and Woodward 1998; Saunderson 2002), they are disproportionately disadvantaged as they strive to balance work life and family life.

Across their time and tenure in academia, women struggle with competing work, family and domestic demands. For many their careers are interrupted by the care ceiling that Grummell et al. (2009) identify as a key reason why women can become 'stuck' at a particular academic level. Research and promotion presuppose the availability of time, financial resources and freedom to dedicate to work and activities that create further career advantages and opportunities. This is time away from home and family and is often not possible for women to pursue. In addition, as Probert (2005) has illustrated, women's ongoing commitment to family as well as gendered expectations regarding the role of women have contributed to the dearth of women in senior academic positions.

The patchwork careers of women as a result of educational and career breaks or fractured patterns of employment due to life circumstances do not easily align with traditional academic career routes and structures. Academic careers have been structured around family ideologies that allow men to pursue an uninterrupted career that can involve long and continuous hours, attendances at international conferences, periods of residence at other universities and relocation for career opportunities (Baruch and Hall 2004; Butterwick and Dawson 2005). School holiday arrangements, ill children or family members, domestic tasks and responsibilities, bearing and rearing children are invisible work that women are expected to juggle alongside their own career aspirations. It is this invisible and unpaid work that obscures the reality of many women's lives as mothers, carers and partners (Deem 2003).

For Indigenous women and ethnic minority women, obligations to family and community are rarely considered as integral to their work both inside and outside the academy (Essed 2000). Shirley, an Indigenous academic spoke about how:

> This university gets a great deal of mileage out of me. I work inside the place for Indigenous students and staff and work outside of the place with Indigenous communities. But it's not that straightforward. I can't separate what I do here with what I do out there. Each impacts on the other. But it also takes a lot of time. And sometimes it is time to sit and listen, to wait ... and I just have to laugh. I was asked how many hours this took so it could be on my workload. How do you count the silences?

An invisible aspect of managing the self as a leader is managing personal and family responsibilities so that they do not interrupt the workplace. Many women commented that there was an underlying expectation that management work could interrupt home life. Louise, a senior leader, indicated she was tired of 'greedy managers' who 'expected me to be mobile, flexible, accommodating, responsible and responsive' in the workplace but did not 'seem to imagine that I might want them to be flexible and accommodating so that I might be able to cope with the dual demands of work and my family. It did not seem to enter their heads.' Indeed, Sue (SL) highlighted the shrinking family and personal time that she had available:

> I was prepared for long hours in this job. But I was not prepared for the almost relentless intrusion into my own time. I stay back, I take projects home, I am constantly on email and the phone. But you know, I don't

spend time at work juggling my domestic life. But I spend whole chunks of my domestic life managing my work, managing my life really.

An enduring frustration observed by Lorna (SL) was that:

when I mention that I am duty-free, it means my children are with their father, when my [male] colleagues mention duty free, they mean what they pick up at the airport on their way back from another international trip.

The above vignettes from Louise, Sue and Lorna indicate that women experience working and being at work differently from their male colleagues. The male model of working (Collinson and Hearn 1996) included long and unpredictable hours, geographical mobility and meetings outside formal hours. These demands are not without significant challenge to women's working lives as they attempt to reconcile career and family aspirations. Lorna remarked that:

It seems to me that women tend to be concerned most of all about work–life balance … yeah, we juggle this … and yeah, the suggestion is that we are the ones with the imbalance that needs to be righted. But does anyone think to ask – why is it this way? – why does this place [the university] expect we balance the imbalance?

This continual balancing act highlights contradictions between discourses of the modernized university that promotes the need for flexible workers and flexible work arrangements while on the other hand demands longer hours and intensified work practices. What exists is a gendered freedom from responsibility that, as the above extract demonstrates, is unproblematic for those who benefit from it. The work of Liff and Ward (2001) concluded that many women in middle management roles are not easily able to reconcile the culture and long hours required of senior managers with their own life circumstances. The inference is that the ideal academic is a dedicated individual who advances their career by undertaking whatever work and hours are required (Acker and Armenti 2004; Bailyn 2003: Benschop and Brouns 2003). The unstated expectations are that life choices are the responsibilities of the individual to manage and that unpaid overtime is required. This is evident in the following comment by Cecilia (SL):

I had always thought that university management was for me and I made a conscious choice to go down this pathway. I liked seeing other women be successful in these roles, get a national profile for their work and make real changes in universities. But what I really did not know about was the overwhelming commitment to work. Work just never stops. But it was relentless, it was every day. It never seemed to stop. But I just thought I had to cope better, to show I could do the job. I wanted to do a good job.

This extract illustrates Cecilia's desire to be a 'good' manager through long hours and a relentless commitment to her job. As one of the few women at a senior level in her university she felt she had to be seen to be present, to be visible doing work, but could not make visible the toll this exacted. Cecilia had actively sought promotion but was unprepared for the demands made of her beyond the working day. She did venture to suggest that 'I will give this up any day now, the demands are just too much'.

There appears to be an institutional expectation that women are 'there for others' and responsible for the emotional wellbeing of colleagues as well as the wider organization (Acker 1994). Ultimately, because women may have responsibilities for children and the care of others, there is a presumption that they have a partial commitment to the organization. Although women may engage in the same roles and responsibilities as their male colleagues, they are subject to different expectations about what they should do (Wajcman 1998). Accordingly, relegating women to minor roles and offering them temporary or limited access to senior leadership roles are ways to locate troubling women (Blackmore 1999) on the periphery until their commitment has been proved. The marked absence of women in senior positions and the marked presence of women in part-time, sessional or fixed-term roles send a clear signal that the academy is deeply gendered. But the surface impression that is presented is that of an institution deeply committed to inclusion. Behind this illusion is the reality of a low tolerance for difference, a strong commitment to conformity and institutional cultures that solidify hierarchical relations of power.

Family and career aspirations appear to be incompatible in greedy organizations (Blackmore and Sachs 2007) that require more than a full-time commitment to work. Indeed, there has been an increase in management prerogative and a decline in family-friendly hours of work, as Cecilia points out. The flexibility now demanded of workers, particularly those in senior roles, has meant that employers have the greater flexibility, not workers (Connell 2006).

Implicitly and frequently senior roles are linked with full-time work thus making it difficult, if not impossible, for women in part-time work to actively compete for promotion to this level (Blackwell 2001; Hakim 2000; Schein 2007). Many of the women interviewed expressed frustration and disappointment that there was a marked lack of opportunity for part-time staff and that there was a certain level of organizational ambivalence about their role:

> I wanted to sign up for courses, for training that I knew would enhance my skills and get me to where I wanted to go. But they all seemed to be held at times when I was not at work, in the school holidays. I asked about shifting dates but was told the holidays were good times as most academics were free from teaching then. When I said that school holidays were no good either, the person on the end of the phone just sighed. I took this to mean I was being difficult, that I was troublesome.
>
> (Sue, SL)

I did apply for a full-time position. I knew I had a really good CV and would have interviewed well. But just before the advertised date for short-listing, I got a call from someone in Human Resources. They asked if I knew the role was full time. I indicated I was interested in discussing possibilities with the Selection Committee. The person then just said 'if we wanted someone part time we would have advertised for part time'. I felt so deflated. I withdrew the application rather than be told I was not good enough to be shortlisted. I could have contested this, but I did not have the energy. I did not want to be labelled a troublemaker either.

(Pam, SL)

In both of these narratives Sue and Pam are located as organizational problems due to their part-time status. There does not appear to be any attempt to recon-cile their employment status with any commitment to gender equity or the diversification of the workforce. Both women are given the clear message that their contribution is limited and subsequently their future aspirations are limited. In these two examples workplace dynamics conspired to limit oppor-tunity for advancement (Chesterman and Ross-Smith 2006). Furthermore, Sue and Pam label themselves as 'troublesome' or potentially a 'troublemaker' if they question the organizational status quo. That neither was the typical worker, a full-time worker, situated them as trouble for the organization that could not adequately respond to their career aspirations and needs. This is exemplified by Mumford and Rumball (1999: 4) who argue that:

There is tremendous pressure on women to show their willingness to compete and take on leadership roles. This puts women in a very difficult position – on the one hand under pressure to apply for senior management positions, yet aware of the consequences to career prospects and self-esteem of being repeatedly unsuccessful and hence labelled potentially as unable to carry out leadership roles.

Both Sue and Pam are cast as neither the ideal employee nor the ideal manager as they appear unable to conform to organizational norms (Collin-son and Hearn 1996). It was as if both women were initially invisible to the organization and their attempts to challenge the status quo were seen as an infringement (Gherardi 1996). They were made to feel uncomfortable, that they did not belong. Sue and Pam were implicitly given the message that they were troublesome and troublemakers. Both women experienced a level of negative visibility and were viewed with suspicion as they were seen as uncommitted to their professional roles (Cohn 2000). The evocative image that is conjured here is of two women intruders who have attempted to join a group of men (McIntosh 1985). Sue talked about how she felt 'swallowed up' and of her discomfort at 'being made to feel I was not committed to the university'.

What did seem possible for some senior women was to negotiate a reduction in working hours once a senior management role was secured. In Lillian's (SL) experience:

> I have always worked full time. My partner looks after our family and home and he has always worked part time. But when my mother became ill, I wanted to take on the carer's role. I became the home worker, that's what we called it so that neither of us thought that this work was less because it was not paid. Anyway, I was the home worker and I was able to negotiate a 0.4 reduction. So I was at home two days and in the office three days. To be honest, I think I was lucky. The university needed me and possibly thought I might resign or go elsewhere if they did not give me the time. Yes, I know they had to, that's the law now. But there is a huge gap between wanting to ask, actually asking, and then getting approval. Sometimes just asking can put you in a vulnerable position and you kind of feel that your colleagues think you are asking for special treatment.

The decision to be the 'home worker' was less onerous for Lillian as she had a partner who was an active parent, who undertook the majority of home-work and who was willing to take on full-time paid work. Lillian was acutely aware that her skills and expertise were in demand and was able to negotiate a change to her work for a specified period of time. Nevertheless she was anxious that her colleagues thought she was asking for preferential treatment and her own sense of her vulnerability was apparent. This example highlights the constant defining and redefining of their work that women undertake (Fournier and Kelemen 2001) and the complex interplay of work and non-work factors (Madsen 2008; Raddon 2002).

Women in formal academic leadership positions remain predominantly single, divorced or sole parents compared to their male counterparts (Blackmore and Sachs 2007; David and Woodward 1998) or more likely to have retired husbands or partners who work from home (Acker and Feuerverger 1997). Women appear to be disadvantaged by gender, particularly motherhood, while fatherhood is not regarded as harming academic careers (Deem 2003). Women with children are subject to contradictory discourses of 'good mother' and 'successful academic' (Raddon 2002). Regardless, women with and without children are expected to behave in motherly ways and evoke a gender of caring in their professional work (Fitzgerald and Wilkinson 2010).

Conclusion

There is an illusion around the data that show women's participation across the academic hierarchy. While there has been some shift in numbers of women at senior levels, in the main, women remain overly represented at lower levels (as lecturers), and under-represented at senior (as professors) and executive levels (as deans, PVCs, DVCs and VCs). However, 'counting' women in is a form of redistributive politics that does not alter privilege *within* the academy (Acker and Armenti 2004). Indigenous women, ethnic minority women and women of colour continue to be significantly absent from universities and university management (Davidson 1997).

Careers are linked with life stages that are a series of transitions from early adulthood through to retirement (Butterwick and Dawson 2005). Although this might point to the suggestion that careers can follow a predetermined path, the reality is that careers are less predictable and increasingly disorderly. For example, many women report that they have obtained various jobs as a result of following their partner or life changes such as divorce or becoming widowed, and that they had rarely planned for promotion (Acker 1990; Ledwith and Manfredi 2000). Thus, women's career paths tend to be patchwork and frequently marked by serendipities such as relocation, restructuring and replacing colleagues who have temporarily vacated their positions.

Those women with family obligations and responsibilities describe their ascendancy to senior positions as accidental (Rose 1998) rather than as a personal or professional strategy. The notion that women's roles revolve around the care of children and family provides convenient stereotypes for seeing women without children as non-conformists. Primarily because women undertake work such as the care of students and academic colleagues (Wyn *et al.* 2000), they can be diverted from traditional academic career paths – paths that are both formalized and normalized through mechanisms such as performance appraisals and promotions processes. Evidence from a number of studies further suggests that women do not apply for promotion too quickly as they risk being seen as pushy and overambitious (Brooks and Mackinnon 2001; Heward 1999; Ledwith and Manfredi 2000). The dominant picture that emerges is that high workloads, high levels of scrutiny of colleagues as well as high levels of institutional accountability to peers can render management a deeply unattractive option for senior women. Managerial environments in higher education reinforce rather than reduce gender inequalities.

Women who move into leadership roles not only learn how to adapt to the prevailing masculinist culture, they learn how to strategically manage their positioning as the organizational 'other' (Probert 2005). First, this involves a tactical distancing from institutional housekeeping roles that require levels of nurturing and mothering of students and staff. Second, a level of resistance to stereotypical assumptions of women's soft and caring leadership styles is required. The risk that this poses, however, is that being seen to be tough and assertive might provoke a level of exclusion from female colleagues precisely because being 'one of the boys' is seen as a rejection of being 'one of the girls'. Being female, manager and colleague can be professionally and personally challenging and can simultaneously evoke feelings of isolation, loneliness and ambiguity about gender performance at work (Devine *et al.* 2011). Third, women undertake a level of self-regulation in terms of taking time away from work for family and caring responsibilities so that their commitment to the organizational cannot be called into question. Finally, as the organizational 'other', women can make productive use of this positioning and open up the momentum for change (Wyn *et al.* 2000).

Chapter 4

Women leading

In this chapter I outline the dynamics and dilemmas women leaders face. I examine the extent to which a leadership game and its gendered rules exist. The rules of the game are seldom devised by women and consequently they must learn them in order to survive in academia. Interactions between women may not always be positive and self-affirming. Rather than being accepted or celebrated for moving into senior roles, women leaders are punished for violating scripts about desirable femininity. Importantly this chapter draws together voices of Indigenous women and highlights the challenges they face as they encounter institutions and the operation of White privilege.

Introduction

For many women universities are inhospitable places. Yet many women derive pleasure from their work as leaders and provide a level of assurance to women in the early and mid career stages that leadership is a possibility.

Women lead in positive, powerful and affirming ways. Women's tendency to be collaborative, empowering, nurturing and facilitative works to their advantage as they seek to build networks and alliances across the institution. These networks and alliances can be mobilized to support women as well as agitate for change (Barry *et al.* 2007). Crucially, narratives from their female colleagues highlight the impact of leaders who subvert the managerialist imperative (Thomas and Davies 2002) and work for and on behalf of other women. As the voices in this chapter highlight, managing the management (Bendl and Schmidt 2012) is important if leadership by/for/among women is to gain traction.

Interventions such as mentoring and professional development programmes (Devos 2008) as well as informal networks (Coleman 2011; Morley 1999) can play a crucial role in the recruitment and retention of women in higher education. Opportunities for networking can negate feelings of loneliness and isolation and provide a way to tap into the institutional grapevine and a collegial forum in a safe environment. McCarthy (2004: 92) describes how women-only networks offer women a 'space to breathe, build confidence and give voice to their concerns'. A serendipitous advantage networks and informal connections offer is that the rules of the academic leadership game can be openly identified and discussed. Couching this as an advantage, Colleen (SL) suggested that 'men can be threatened by women's networking because they don't know when we meet and what we talk about'. She then added:

> universities are threatening places for women and that's why networks are important. In my last place I set up a Senior Women's Network. My [male] dean used to say to me – 'you're off to your coven of women then?' The irony was he'd trot off every Friday to the University Club and called it 'networking'.

How then can women redraw the management boundaries?

Dynamics and dilemmas

Universities are replete with 'strong imprints of masculine domination' (Alvesson 2002: 11). These imprints have two particular forms: given the numerical dominance of men at senior levels, women appear to be out of place, strangers in the landscape. Second, routine organizational activities are premised on male and masculine ways of working (Priola 2007) thereby reinforcing normative expectations. Women leaders must navigate and negotiate the masculine terrain of leadership. The dilemma that exists is whether women's aspirations are inextricably linked with a subconscious desire to belong to the dominant institutional group, their senior male colleagues (Gherardi and Poggio 2007). Sue (SL) highlighted this when she revealed that 'being at the "big boys' table"' and 'knowing what was going on' motivated her to apply for a leadership role.

Despite the rhetoric of inclusion that circulates in higher education, women are repeatedly cast as the 'other' and outsiders in this dominant male world. How then do they find a space for leadership? Do they continually reaffirm themselves as a counter to male discourses? How do they talk about and engage in their work? Do they learn to 'fit in' or do they play a different game (Bryans and Mavin 2003)? Why do women want or need to play these gendered games (Acker 2012)? Colleen (SL) summed this up when she said:

> But you know, it's not just the blokes who hate not knowing the rules. Women hate the games other women play just as much. Maybe it's not about the game but that women actually think it's important to get involved in playing games.

Previous research studies have shown that significant proportions of women academics appear to be reticent about applying for senior positions (Probert 2005; Ross-Smith and Chesterman 2009). What this does mean is that those women who wish to move up to a more senior role can be in high demand, as Adele (SL) recalls:

> I had a lot of approaches from various universities around Australia.... There is not a lot of leadership talent around and so when they are looking, there is a very small pool to look at and there are lots of really good opportunities.

Similarly, Margaret (SL) outlined that in her experience:

> Most of my career has been via people asking me to apply for things ... I would be working away on a job and someone would notice and I would be headhunted. I've been able to make choices about it of course ... I've had a very varied career, but basically I've been invited into new positions and I've thought I'd quite like to do that. Moving [here], again I was headhunted ... I've been identified as someone who could do a particular job and been asked to do it. It's been a progression.

There appears to be no hesitation by either Adele or Margaret that they had the necessary skills and academic background to take up a new role. Being encouraged to apply or being 'headhunted' was an important signifier that they were strong candidates. These comments resonate with previous research across public and private sector organizations that showed women benefited from exposure to a supportive climate and direct encouragement to pursue career opportunities (Bagilhole and Goode 2001; Currie *et al.* 2002; Eveline 2004).

Making space for leadership is complex and demanding work. For Indigenous women theirs is a self-conscious struggle (Collins 1998) to offer formal and informal leadership from the intersections of ethnicity and gender. Many are first in their field and must create and walk a path that has not existed. Indigenous women carry the expectations of family and community. As an Indigenous woman, Aroha was conscious that she had been successful in obtaining various promotions based on her reputation and the specific portfolio:

> I've moved around a bit. Mostly the jobs I have had are linked with Māori aspirations. You know improving access and opportunity, supporting Māori students and staff, setting up programmes. For me there is a lot of trust in me. *Whanau* (family) and *iwi* (tribal group) are looking to me for change to happen. But it takes time to *korero* (talk) with *whanau* and *iwi* and then talk inside this place [university] to Pākehā colleagues and Pākehā committees. It's double talk for me.

Alienation and isolation mark the experiences of Indigenous women. This point is underscored by Myra who pointed out that:

being in a White place is difficult. No one uses the term White, but they are talking about White. White students, White staff. I am constantly reminded this [the university] is a White place and about White ways.

She went on to say that she wondered whether 'this place was for me. There is nothing of me here. I sometimes think I don't belong. I know the rules, I just don't like them. But I have to play by their rules.' The rules, privileged ways of thinking, acting, speaking and behaving (Collins 1991; Roman and Eyre 1997) were, as Myra had earlier indicated, 'White ways' that were not 'my reality, my way of knowing, my way of working'. Lucashenko (1994: 23), an Indigenous Australian feminist, emphatically talked back in similar ways to White feminists:

> our reality is not your reality. What you call patriarchy, I call one aspect of colonization; for all their commonalities, for all your hoping and wishing it, our oppressions are not interchangeable. Whether you like it or not, as a White Australian woman you are at the root of my Indigenous problem.

For Myra knowing the institutional culture ('the rules') and its expectations implied knowing what was explicitly and implicitly expected of her. Myra was well aware that as an Indigenous woman she 'stuck out. I have to know what to do and do it better. I have to be better. It's the only way.' 'To be better' and 'do better', Myra had to exceed expectations of her White male and female colleagues. But these rules were alienating as they are framed within White cultural and masculinist traditions (Arya 2012; Collins 1998; Moreton-Robinson 2000). As both Myra and Pat have signalled, Whiteness imparts invisible advantages to both men and women and accordingly, dominant White cultures remain the norm. As Moreton-Robinson (2000: 389) points out:

> despite discussions of difference ... relations between Indigenous and white women are analysed through the white woman's filtered lens which is blind to the way in which white race privilege manifests itself in and through these relations.

The notion of 'colonization [as] a living process' (Moreton-Robinson 2000: 2) is evident in Pat's recollection of a discussion that occurred in late January 2011. She remarked on the alienation that she felt when 'they [colleagues] talk about Australia Day [26 January]. They talk about what they are going to do on the day off. But they don't stop to think what that day might mean for me, for my people, for country.' For both women, the university did not feel a culturally safe place:

> If you're not an Indigenous person, you go to work and you go home and that's fine. But with us, you go to work, what we do at work – especially if you are involved with Indigenous students, you know – what we do here

impacts on a community. We can't just be at work and then be at home. I bring home and bring community to work, I bring work to home. But going home reconnects me.

(Pat)

For Myra too 'going home' and 'forgetting about it for a while' was one of the coping mechanisms that she employed. This very much resonates with hooks (1989: 42) who refers to these safe spaces as 'homeplace':

a safe place where Black people could affirm one another, and by so doing, heal many of the wounds inflicted by racist domination ... we can make homeplace that space where we return for renewal and self-recovery, where we can heal our wounds and become whole.

Knowing who she was, where she came from and her connections with land were all important for Aroha. Her feelings of alienation began:

When I was interviewed for my job they asked me all about what I had done previously, how it all contributed to this new career direction I wanted to take [senior management]. They also asked me the usual questions about my vision, my leadership style and my experience with budgets, with people, with policy. Not once, not once did they ask about my *whakapapa* [genealogy], about who I was and where I had come from. I should have known. Not even a *mihi* [greeting] at the beginning, no chance to tell about me.

These stories reveal that the unpreparedness of an institution to reframe their strategies to be more inclusive is deeply hurtful for Indigenous women such as Myra, Pat and Aroha. However, universities were quite prepared to co-opt their presence for marketing purposes. As Pat said 'my face was plastered all over publications. I think it was some kind of statement about the kind of place the university was.' Using Pat to promote the university produced an image of the organization as demographically diverse and culturally inclusive (Battiste 2000; Jones 2004). Barbara emphasized that as an Indigenous woman she was acutely aware of the need to be visible, but that this visibility took several forms:

As an Indigenous academic I need to be visible in the community, for them to know that I am here [the university] working for *whanau* [family], for *iwi* [people]. As an academic I need to be visible at conferences, in organizations like NZARE [New Zealand Association for Research in Education]. Pākehā [White] women just get to be visible in their academic world. But I have *whanau, iwi*, university and academic community. And here [the university] I am visible as a Māori academic, as a Māori woman. I can't separate it out.

This account speaks to the multiple identities and intersectionality of identities that Indigenous women confront (Davis 2008; Fitzgerald 2010). This further emphasizes the invisible boundaries that surround Indigenous women and their continual struggles to be visible. White women may well encounter boundaries surrounding male and masculine privilege but, as Barbara's story shows, to be visible she must transcend boundaries between herself and Pākehā men and Pākehā women. It is a moot point whether, given the accounts from Indigenous women, they can survive the power structures and practices of universities (Arya 2012).

Clubs and networks

A constant theme has been the male networks (boys' clubs) that work to advantage men in academic institutions. These networks can be formal, informal or personal but they are systematically linked with male privilege and patronage. Male-dominated networks are a form of gatekeeping that have a dual function to exclude and control while simultaneously distributing resources, information and opportunities (Husu 2001). As Sue (SL) commented:

> I continue to be agitated by the big boys at the table and their reluctance to hear what I have to say. They don't listen. I can tell. You know, shrug of the shoulders, facial expressions. In fact I see them put their heads down, check emails when I am talking and sometimes there is even a murmur of another conversation. I thought I had the support of a few male colleagues but they seem to side with the other blokes. I feel like I am always in competition for the space to be heard. I just can't get on with my job some days.

It would seem that for Sue the price of membership at the 'big boys' table' was conformity to masculine norms through her silence and enforced marginality at meetings (Marshall 1995; Olssen 2000). Marion (SL) mentioned that she too had experienced being dismissed:

> I think men automatically undervalue women. If you say something they don't take it as seriously. I don't know if it's the way you talk, or the tone of voice, I don't know but there is something about it where you are more easily dismissed.

Colleen (SL) described ways in which the boys' club worked at her university:

> It's complicated, but I believe that the boys' club, the mates' club absolutely exist and that they are quite powerful and for female leaders that can be difficult to negotiate around. Power relationships are quite difficult sometimes.... Sometimes that boys' club is intimidating. The boys' club

is hard to define, but if … if you are socially interacting after a meeting what happens is that the males are physically together talking about the kinds of topics that women are often not interested in, you know, the football. I'm not slightly interested and find it hard to be in those kinds of conversations. It's like if you are not in the inner circle you are not taken as much notice of than if you were in that club and able to have those conversations.

Women-only networks counter the exclusionary and perceived advantages that men are thought to derive from networking. For women, networks offer a level of support, friendship and contacts. Perriton (2006) has pointed out, women-only networks are likely to be perceived as being less powerful simply because they are women-only. Such networks can be denigrated as 'mothers' meetings' (Perriton 2006: 100). Women may elect not to join women-only networks as they do not afford access to powerful male networks. A further disadvantage is that these networks are generally formed within institutions and work to assimilate women into the dominant male culture and to fit with organizational norms (Chesterman and Ross-Smith 2006; Devos 2008; McKeen and Bujaki 2007). In multiple instances, mentoring suits the purposes of the institution precisely because it 'activates the operation of technologies of self' which women take up 'to manage themselves as women academic workers' (Devos 2005: 194). As de Vries (2005: 11) puts it, mentoring programmes teach women to 'play the game'.

The potential of mentoring programmes lies in benefits such as 'handing down knowledge, maintaining culture, supporting talent and securing leadership', but 'traditionally, the mentoring relationship has been framed in a language of paternalism and dependency and stems from power dependant, hierarchical relationships aimed at maintaining the status quo' (Darwin 2000: 198). As women move to more senior roles they become isolated from the majority of their colleagues and networks become a critical form of support. Eveline (2004) has described women-only networks as necessary for companionship and comfort, rather than as a means to connect powerful women with one another. Importantly, networks offer opportunity to create a safe space in which competing demands, external commitments such as caring responsibilities and insecurities can be disclosed and discussed without judgement. Zoe (academic) summed this up when she said:

Men network differently from women and women have to be much more strategic about how they network. We just don't have time to waste…. Our style is more collaborative, so we get together about an issue or an idea. Or we have a purpose, sometimes we listen to war stories and try and unpack what has happened and what to do. We don't have time to waste, we are not hanging out like the blokes.

Women-only networks do have a role to play in connecting women across an institution, providing a level of support and offering opportunity to share experiences. The power and potential of these networks is accentuated by McCarthy (2004: 11):

> Through their ability to connect women with other women, networks disrupt patterns of social connectivity at work that have for so long privileged men, and in doing so provide a new way to alter the balance of power between the sexes.

For Wanda (academic) networks were an important way to organize women across her discipline:

> I am very much about getting together for events. We organize a movie night for women in my discipline, not just from the university but from other universities. Once a month we get together. It's a networking thing that we do. We take it in turns to organize it. There is about ten of us and about six of us usually turn up, so that is our discipline from different universities coming together. The men don't often realize how well we know each other. They often introduce us to each other at conferences. We play it down because we don't necessarily want them to know.

Wanda's narrative emphasizes ways in which women informally work to support one another and the consequent strength in 'coming together', connecting across a discipline and institutions, and forging friendships. Hence, this network is both professional and social. It is a network known only to the participants and while inclusive of women, their male colleagues are not apprised of its existence. In this instance, solidarity between women works to create ties between women and claim the network as women's knowledge.

Women's presence in the world of men is conditional on their willingness to modify their behaviour and become more like men (Wajcman 1998). Interviewed in her first year as a DVC, Pam asked 'Do I join the male game or do I challenge it?' Ryan and Haslam (2005) argue that opening up leadership to women does not necessarily make the playing field any more level, as Pam discovered. But, as Pam further commented 'I don't want to be one of the boys even if I am in the boys' club, but it's very lonely at the top'. Similarly Sue (SL) revealed that 'I am very aware that women look to me for leadership. They look to see that I work differently to my male colleagues ... that I offer alternatives to how leadership is carried out in this place.' But she recognized that 'I have to get on with my male colleagues too. And sometimes that just means being like them to get the job done.' For both Sue and Pam the management game was stressful and highly regulated around masculine behaviours (Wajcman 1998). To be able to play the management game required a conscious and unconscious set of practices to be internalized and routinized.

Both Sue and Pam were conscious they were the sole women at their level and that, as recent arrivals to the role and university, they were suddenly visible for the first time. Both were aware of the need to establish their 'fit' within a new organization, both were aware they needed to establish their own credibility, and both wanted to be involved in wider institutional change and establish their own ways of working and their own networks. Sue and Pam's reflections pinpoint the distinctively masculinist and male-oriented culture of universities (Whitehead 1998). Women who advance to senior levels find out just how narrowly male-dominated universities continue to be (Blackmore and Sachs 2007). Changing the organizational status quo becomes more difficult if women face this chilly climate (Maranto and Griffin 2011) and opt to either evacuate the role or leave the organization (Kloot 2004).

A number of staff offered their perceptions about Sue and Pam. For example, Linda commented that:

> Sue has been here for about a year. I think she spent most of the first few months visiting people and talking with people. Change is needed in this place but I am not sure it will get done. I'm not sure Sue has a thick enough skin to cope with the testosterone of the senior management team. While no one says it openly, I think they bullied the last woman DVC out, so why not a Dean? She's in the headlights for sure. And if she leaves then they'll whisper that she was not up to the job anyway … but they brought her in to clean up their mess.

In her role Sue was exposed to intense scrutiny and criticism (Ryan and Haslam 2005). There is a clear mandate for change but staff remain unsure as to whether she has a 'thick enough skin' to cope with her masculinist colleagues. It would seem that Sue is in a precarious position and if she does not succeed she will be blamed, not the senior management team. The prediction that Sue will leave if she is 'not up to the job' will then restore the gender order (Gherardi and Poggio 2007).

Carol (academic) who reported to Pam offered her view:

> Pam has a vision about what she wants to get done and she really wants us all to be involved. It's exciting really. She wants to get on and get some changes in place. She's really approachable and she really listens. But I am not sure who is listening to her. I've been to a few meetings and she is often the last one asked for her opinion. There is a clear hierarchy going on. The VC always asks the Dean of Medicine first for his view, then Science and so on. Then he turns to his DVCs and the pecking order seems to be Research, International and then Pam. It's pretty obvious to me there is a pecking order.

What Carol has identified here is an unconscious hierarchical order in operation based on academic disciplines as well as gender. While this unconscious bias might not be immediately evident, it works as a form of exclusionary tactic. The tacit message being communicated is that men talk and women listen; or indeed, while men talk, women listen and when women talk, men talk. Evident from this passage is the cultural association of power and authority with masculinity. In this situation the masculinity of power (Charles and Davies 2000) worked to limit Pam. In the words of Sinclair (1998: 109), 'even before they open their mouths or act, men are likely to be endowed with power and the potential for leadership'. What Carol's observation reveals is the direct association of organizational power and authority and leadership with masculinized ways of knowing.

In terms of the observed 'pecking order', as Pam was not a male leader she did not feature in the hierarchy. To fit would have required her to adopt masculine leader behaviours, to assert herself into the natural speaking order of the meeting. The equally unappealing options Pam faced were to either remain silent, thereby reinforcing her non-leader status, or interrupt and not conform to gendered expectations. She was at risk of simultaneously being cast as a non-leader and a non-woman. Acceptance required a demonstration of masculinity and a suppression of femininity (Acker 1990; Eagly and Carli 2007). The subtext of this example was women as 'other' and male as the norm (Bendl 2008).

The experiences and perceptions of Sue and Pam as recounted by their two female colleagues centre on what each woman 'lacks'. That is, the two women 'lack' masculine characteristics and qualities. In the case of Sue, she has a 'lack' of testosterone and is unable to garner support from the senior management team. Accordingly their power to be acknowledged, listened to or speak is reduced and their performance is viewed as something 'other' than leadership (Schnurr 2008). Herein lies a paradox: while modern organizations applaud the leader who is sensitive and expressive, emotionally intelligent, a good communicator and listener with highly developed people skills, it is striking that there is no space inside organizations for these skills and attributes to take precedence over the perceived behaviours reported by Linda and Carol.

Organizations are intensely preoccupied with defining themselves in relation to lack. For example, university strategic plans are resplendent with their deficits be they research productivity and research income targets, quality improvements, financial outcomes, student retention and success rates, or world rankings. Progress, improvement and measurement contained in these plans are focused on future aspirations and desires and a future and better organization. Leaders and leadership are not immune from these discourses as order, logic, direction and rationality are considered necessary to bring about organizational performance and improvement (Blackmore and Sachs 2007).

Being good

Those women who were seen as strong and authoritative in their own right faced accusations from their female colleagues that they were either 'one of the boys' (Keller and Moglen 1987) or 'playing a game' (Bryans and Mavin 2003). An illustrative comment comes from Mary, a senior lecturer who observed the following about her dean (Alana):

> I don't really know Alana. I have never even spoken to her. I see her around and we hear about how in control she is. She's pretty successful at what she does, she's pretty focused on results and pretty driven if you ask me. It's probably hard being in a management job like that but I think she has learned how to play the game. She's been around a long time and I think she knows what to say, when to say it and who to say it to. But I think it's also about what her male colleagues want to hear.

It would seem from this vignette that Alana has been assimilated into the organization. She has learned not to antagonize her male colleagues and, similarly, they have become adept at protecting and promoting their own interests. Alana knows the rules and confirmed that:

> I've been in this place too long to not know the rules, you know, the rules of engagement. It may take longer than I expect but I get things done eventually. I don't get offside with my [male] colleagues. There's no point. They will just wear me down and win in the end. It's about knowing what will work and what will not, playing to your strengths and keeping your cool.

There is clear imagery in this passage of winning not losing, knowing the rules and not transgressing, being good and not being punished and a willingness to tolerate unequal relationships. In this example leadership is related to achievement, power and compromise. Reading against the grain here, it is further possible that Alana 'plays the game' precisely because, in order to succeed, she must be accepted as an equal and this ultimately means a level of sacrifice. She must construct a self that is not feminine and project herself as subordinate to male expectation (Acker 1990). Being a leader implicitly requires Alana to act in certain ways, to be seen to be capable of doing the job, and to fit in with the organizational culture (Sinclair 2004). Alana was playing a range of roles in order to survive. There is little or no ambivalence here about what was required: accept the role, speak and act when required, or be deprived of male patronage. In other words, Alana was being a 'good' girl and not rattling any patriarchal cages.

The earlier accounts about Sue and Pam and this latter vignette from Alana highlight challenges women face: the underlying sense of 'lack' because they are not male, the cumulative effect of organizational power, limited opportunities and being relegated to the periphery until they have proved their worth and commitment. There are real costs to women that these 'rules of engagement' (Alana) demand. Ironically, precisely what men fear is that their own logic and reasoning will be exposed if alternative ways of working and priorities that stand in contradiction to their organizational realities are promoted. A nuanced reading of these accounts suggests that Sue, Pam and Alana are engaged in a balancing act – that they are performing in order to reconcile their dualistic positions as 'women' and as 'competent leaders'. Each woman attempted to downplay her gender identity by projecting an image that is tolerable to her male peers. The net result was that the male-dominated culture of the organization remains intact.

Sue's, Pam's and Alana's narratives indicate that there are repeating patterns established by their male colleagues (Eagly and Carli 2007). As newcomers each woman observed that masculine leadership behaviours were valued yet were disappointed that their own way of working was less valued. What seemed evident here is that male colleagues held beliefs about how women ought to *ideally* behave (Barreto and Ellemers 2010). As a result, behaviour that deviates from gendered stereotypes is, on the one hand, unexpected, and on the other, risky. Simply put, the good corporate citizen does good and looks good. For those who do not wish to play the game, but want to change the rules of the game, leadership is dangerous terrain.

Doing good

Women's performances, their emotions, appearance, language and behaviours are highly scrutinized and interpreted differently by others because of their gender. The gaze is particularly intense on ambitious and successful women. Those women who move into senior roles are highly vulnerable to criticism if they are seen to be acting too hard or too soft – that is, acting like a man or acting like a woman respectively (Blackmore 1999). In Lillian's view:

> I think women do things differently, they approach things differently, and I think one of the challenges is that we are so used to the way men do it that we don't notice it.... People expect women to be different. They might expect them to be more caring and consultative, so if you don't quite hit the mark then they probably label you as autocratic. You are judged differently. People don't like women making decisions and being in positions of making decisions.

Assuming any formal leadership or management role instantly projects women into the institutional spotlight and the public gaze. The immediate dilemma women confront is the gendered expectation that they will lead in particular ways. Joce (SL) recalled that, in her experience, 'because I am a woman people expect me to be really, really consultative and they are shocked. I am not as consultative as some men I work with. That can be difficult for some people.'

Jane (academic), who had experience working with three different women leaders, offered the following summary of her perceptions:

There would be three women leaders I can think of. I suppose what I am struck by with those three women they were entirely different. So the first one was, I suppose, a more motherly kind of leadership. It was a fairly nice environment, she went for harmony. I wasn't up close enough to know how good she was at the hard stuff. Then the next one was, well I would say a thinking type, entrepreneurial, overseas a lot of the time, very directive but very competent and straight. I didn't have any problems with her, [and] think she was fine. She just wasn't here a lot. The one we have now is a wonderful combination, really I find her very impressive. She manages to be both warm and competent. I've had personal dealings with her with a difficulty I've been through recently and I was just really impressed by the way she listened so well. She listened and she was quite strategic. I think she is excellent and people generally around the place tend to think she is excellent.

Two of the women in this example were recognized for their all-giving and constantly available leadership. This recurrent theme of caring is woven throughout Jane's narrative and indicates the extent to which staff expect and appreciate this approach but also the professional toll (Acker 2012). A follow-up comment from Jane was that the entrepreneurial woman was 'aiming for the top and so didn't really have a lot of time to put into encouraging staff below her that couldn't directly feed into her aspirations'. These three examples mirror the sexual division of labour and gendered parenting roles within a family. Women care and engage in pastoral work but ultimately, as Jane's narrative indicates, this caring and nurturing is not highly valued in the managerial context (Devine *et al.* 2011; Leathwood 2000).

The family metaphor here is illustrative of ways in which women and their work are conceptualized and operationalized. One woman adopted a 'motherly' role and was 'fairly nice and harmonious'. Her role was not to engage in the 'hard stuff' but to ensure that the staff (family) was content. The inference here is that this woman leader was in a secondary role to the 'father' figure in the family whose authority and responsibilities were 'natural' and legitimate. Women are expected to 'mother' their colleagues, male and female. The metaphor of familial patterns of authority is evident in academia where men are usually seen as the 'master' and head of the household and women the institutional mother-figure (Leathwood 2000; Raddon 2002). This is echoed in Leesa's perception of a woman leader, Penny, with whom she worked:

Penny was expected to look after everyone. She was expected to be kind and nice, and weak and mothering; expected to pick up those roles that are attending to the human needs; behaving like a mother rather than a leader. It's really expected of women.

The expectation that women will behave 'like a mother rather than a leader' is a paternalistic way to control women by seducing them into believing that being caring and protective is 'good' for the recipient as well as 'good' leadership (Blackmore and Sachs 2007; Kerfoot and Knights 2004). In greedy institutions men rely on women to undertake this 'mothering' work as well as a level of institutional housekeeping thereby reinforcing paternalistic organizational patterns (Leathwood 2000).

Adopting familial patterns to describe and confine women's work suggests the operation of a form of paternalistic management (Kerfoot and Knights 1993) whereby family-like relationships reduce tensions and power is exercised by a male authoritative figure. The second woman leader in Jane's narrative was described as 'entrepreneurial', but was distant from the staff. Similar to an absent father, she was overseas a great deal but seen to be 'competent and straight'. Here again is the imagery of the absent figure engaged in important tasks away from the 'home'. In this instance, the competitive work environment requires a level of flexibility to be able to travel and undertake entrepreneurial activities (Clarke and Newman 1997). The third woman leader Jane described adopted a parental way of working through her problem-solving abilities and being 'quite strategic'. That she was deemed to be 'excellent' points to the suggestion that she was able to occupy a managerial subject position yet at the same time maintain a hold on her own values that staff determined were 'excellent'. This is what Prichard and Deem (1999) refer to as wo-managing.

The expectation of 'being good and doing good' is illustrated by Alison's (SL) comments about how she enhanced her profile at a previous institution:

> I was the only woman. It gave me space to show how well I could do the job. I didn't keep a low profile. My women friends in other universities told me to keep my head down, to not be noticed for the wrong things. I've never done wallflower particularly well.... It all worked for me really. The short story. I got the university noticed in the press for all the right things. There were a few stories, photographs, that sort of thing. We looked good, good for the image. Nothing cheers a VC up more than good press I can tell you.

It would seem that being a good academic citizen had worked to Alison's advantage. Crucially she had made the VC happy. In other words, she made the boys look good by doing 'good' herself, acting like a good girl (Bagilhole 1993; Kanter 1993; McCarthy 2004). It would seem too that Alison has been what Gallop (1995) refers to as a 'good-girl feminist'.

Essentially what had occurred here was that Alison derived a level of pleasure from the performative regime which had motivated her to look good, do good and provide evidence of her good works. This example further underscores the behaviours and actions required of women to gain entry and acceptance and to remain in this environment. This necessitates a level of role deviance that reveals incongruities between the masculine managerial role and the female gender role. Women who move into senior management destabilize the gender order. But they cannot win. Women cannot easily reconcile the contradictory demands of being managerial and being feminine (Blackmore 1997; Maddock 1999; Wajcman 1998). The Faustian decision is to behave as a man and reject femininity, or act feminine and be seen as a token manager.

Looking good

The managerialist environment situates leadership at the centre of new structures and practices. This has required leaders to learn a new game centred on a corporate ethos of accountability, fiscal efficiency, targets and outputs, organizational change and a shared commitment to a strategic vision. Leaders are expected to perform against a set of internal expectations and external standards and evaluate their performance against an agreed set of objectives and performance indicators that are codified in performance agreements. The functions, priorities and responsibilities demanded by these new regimes shape and define how leadership is understood and viewed. Emphasis is placed on outcomes and image; being seen to perform matters.

Moving into formal leadership roles can mean a reworking and reimagining of self as well as a repackaging of self to meet the demands of diverse markets, research priorities and institutional objectives. As part of this management of self, academics must promote and project themselves in ways that attract desirable attention to the institution. Being seen to perform is advantageous.

The outward sign of being a leader and the projection of leadership is frequently linked with dress, language and actions. Women in male-dominated contexts such as universities work to moderate aspects of their self-presentation such as dress and language (Blackmore and Sachs 2007) so as to be feminine enough not to meet the rejection of their female colleagues but not so feminine that they will be rejected as leaders. Being male and masculine is not an issue for men (Acker 1990) but for women being female and feminine can be an issue partially informed by gender scripts about how women leaders should act and react and informed by others' perceptions of their actions. Dress is critical to both credibility and image for women in leadership. Careful posture, neat and subdued clothing, minimal make-up and conservative hairstyles denote the capacity to exert a level of self-control and self-management. This external management of self is ostensibly for the male eye that ultimately has the permissible power of seeing how women present and project themselves. This is very much in evidence in the words of Kathleen (SL):

> I experience a high degree of angst before I even get to some of the meetings. Sure, I read the meeting papers, sure I canvas colleagues' views, but what troubles me most is what to wear. I need to look formal, I need to look like I know what I am doing. I am the only woman in the room. I always wear a suit. Sometimes I use a little colour, like a scarf, it helps me feel brighter but then when I see all the men in sombre suits I feel frivolous. It reminded me I was not one of them and never could be.

I remember quite vividly going to a meeting and there were a number of women senior to me there. Most of the men in the room were transfixed by Adele who wore a very tight dress and very high heels. I am not sure what this was all about. I thought it did nothing for women, nothing at all.

(Marion, SL)

Both Kathleen and Marion call attention to the sexualization of women's identity and denigrate either herself or her colleague for the absence of any form of self-regulation in dress. Kathleen in particular has exerted a level of pressure on herself to be able to perform and be seen to perform. Her fear and anxieties mirror the study by Acker and Armenti (2004) that showed the extent to which self-esteem and self-presentation were core concerns for academic women. Wearing a scarf, for Kathleen, was an outward (and colourful) sign that she was not 'one of them', yet always wearing a suit was a marker of her position in the academic hierarchy. But for Kathleen her anxiety and ambivalence about what to wear created a level of uncertainty about how she would be perceived. Her female bodily presence at the meeting was an overt threat to the dominant masculinity in the room.

In contrast, Adele (SL) created a disturbance because of her dress and appearance. She did not minimize her femininity and her physical presence drew the attention of her male colleagues. While this might be read as a moment of heightened male desire or one carrying the implication of sexual availability, this vignette can also be read as a subtle form of control being exerted on Adele. That their gaze was 'transfixed' suggests a concentrated male gaze because of her deviant dress and appearance. Adele refused to act out a predetermined role and this refusal exposed her to sanction via the transfixed gaze of her male colleagues and the criticism of her colleague, Marion. Not only did Marion express a level of embarrassment and derision, she associated these feelings with the possible denigration of women more widely.

Image management was critical to credibility and image for younger women. Julia (academic) remarked that she was 'seen as too young' and that 'in meetings I have to do false serious so I am not overlooked'. For Julia being 'false serious' meant she paid careful attention to her attire as well as her glasses. 'Too frivolous,' she continued, 'and no one pays attention', and this required dressing 'in understated colours, you know, black or dark blue because ... my Head of School (male) told me once too much colour makes me look too casual'. Being too casual was associated with not being taken seriously. Julia was conscious that her subtle dress and appearance marked her as being serious and in control of herself. In this case the logic of performativity (Blackmore and Sachs 2007) required her to be 'false serious'.

Gender, sexuality and the body are integral to the complex technologies of control that exist in organizations. Male sexuality and bodies are invisible because they are normalized but women, because of their hyper-visibility, must exert control over their dress, language and manner so as to not draw attention to their sexuality. In each of the examples cited, women and their body are at risk; at risk of being frivolous and at risk of being sexualized. The men in Kathleen's story conformed to a particular dress code, the sombre suit a symbol of institutionalized practices. Dressing in a suit symbolizes Kathleen's conformity to organizational norms. Adele's clothing and the 'little colour' injected into Kathleen's outfit symbolize a level of opposition.

How women leaders dress for their everyday work, dress for an occasion, or choose to represent themselves through dress can be subjected to intense scrutiny. As Connell (1995) comments, dressing up for men is a form of emphasized femininity. Those women who do not conform to particular dress codes are perceived as a risk. Those whose bodies are neither White nor male, and whose bodies are not clothed in dark suits, white shirts and ties do not fit stereotypic images of the leader. Hughes (2004: 538) identifies the dangers that female managers encounter in their attire as:

> too masculine and she is threatening. Too feminine and she is wimpish. The feminine touch is just a little make-up. Too much and one is the sexual working-class women. None at all and one is of suspect sexuality.

Appropriate attire requires women to conform to institutional norms while simultaneously projecting traditional femininity. Increasingly in the performative environment of universities, the presentation of image as well as a level of self-surveillance about clothing, language and conduct are crucial. Ultimately survival is about image and performance.

Caring and sharing

In the current climate of constant restructuring, redundancies and retirements, the unspoken expectation is that women will undertake a high degree of emotional labour to support their colleagues (Blackmore 1996). Too much care and too much collaboration can be dangerous as they heighten expectations that all women will act in similar ways. A further danger is that women's emotional work will be seen as 'natural' and will therefore be unrecognized and unsupported, yet seen as a positive attribute in those male managers who display a level of emotional awareness (Collinson and Hearn 1994; Connell 2006). In many ways women leaders juggle a quadruple burden of expectations; their public image, job performance, household and family arrangements and as a path-breaker for their female colleagues.

Leadership is emotional work. Leadership involves making judgements about priorities, values, professional relationships and individuals. This emotional work is neverending, tiring and infrequently acknowledged. Primarily it is work that women undertake that may further contribute to the feminization of their labour. The following account by Lillian (SL) underscores this point:

> I had been in the job for about seven months and one of the staff emailed to acknowledge my support for him during a difficult personal time. I remember feeling angry at his words. He told me how none of his previous managers, all male, had ever seemed to care and that I had made a difference. That I cared, that I listened and that I made him feel safe. I had spent considerable time on previous occasions talking with him about his work, his research plans and talking through promotion prospects. I never got emails about those discussions. I was angry, I felt devalued and I thought that nothing I had done mattered until that mothering moment.

This example highlights the disproportionate amount of informal emotional labour expected of women leaders (Acker and Armenti 2004; Morley 1999) and that, unlike the previous male incumbents, Lillian could neither be care-free nor care-less. Her performance was bound up with her primary care work and she was predominantly recognized for her 'mothering moment' rather than as a senior leader. A further element of complexity and contradiction here is that when the perception was that Lillian had 'made a difference', she reinforced the male staff member's own reality and expectation of a female leader.

For both Lillian and the staff member, management and care work were interwoven and there was an unquestioned cultural assumption that Lillian would undertake this work when approached. There appears to be a marked absence of acknowledgement of her previous work and it was only when Lillian engaged in emotional work that there was a degree of recognition of this work. But it is not Lillian as a senior leader who is recognized, but Lillian as a substitute mother and as a primary caregiver of staff. Lillian, as a woman leader, was seen to be acting appropriately by the staff member whose email reinforced her feminine self and caring self that now appeared to fit the environment. A further reading of this incident is that the gendering of her identity created a struggle in Lillian about her own self-perception as well as the perception of the staff member. None of her previous work had 'mattered until that mothering moment'. This incident parallels Jenkins (1996: 21) who suggests that:

> what people think about us is no less important than what we think of ourselves. It is not enough to assert an identity. That identity must be validated (or not) by those with whom we have dealings.

Managing negative emotions such as anger, fear, stress, hurt and alienation is critical to performativity for women leaders (Acker 2012). Women who display such emotions are perceived as negative, unruly and not in control. Emotions such as calmness, caring, conciliation, responsiveness and intuition, warmth and patience are expected of women; to show negative emotions is an outward sign of being non-feminine and non-caring. Women who cry are wimpish (Hughes 2004) and perceived as weak leaders. As Alison (SL) commented:

> You learn really quickly to suppress emotions. I don't get angry, I don't show tears. I have to show I am tough, that I can deal with the stress, the uncertainty. But I do cry, I do rant and I do swear. I just do it in my office, in the car or in my garden.

Alison's story illustrates the extent to which women are expected to productively manage negative and unproductive emotions and the need to create a safe haven for themselves. That Alison has learned to suppress her negative emotions allays any discomfort her colleagues may feel if she is angry or in tears. She was aware that showing her emotions might expose her to criticism and undermine her credibility. For women managers there is a heightened visibility and an overwhelming pressure to perform successfully (Cohn 2000).

Positive emotions such as enthusiasm, collegiality, empathy and so forth are harnessed by organizations as a way to counter any disillusionment or alienation that widespread and uncertain change can cause. As well as managing their own emotions and showing they are in control, women are expected to manage the emotions of their colleagues – to calm, soothe and encourage particularly during times of massive organizational change, disillusionment and alienation. This is particularly evident from an encounter that Judy (SL) recalled:

> I was bruised by the proposed restructuring of the faculty. I did not agree at all with what was being proposed. But I was reminded that I was part of the senior management and that my support was expected. I was trying to deal with my own feelings of frustration and alienation and when I walked into the staff meeting I met a wall of hostility and some very hurt staff. It had been made clear to me that I had to get the buy-in of staff for what was being proposed. I did what I could but I made sure that I gave no indication that I supported the proposal. I tried to remain neutral, I tried to remain calm.

In terms of her own survival, Judy was left with little choice but to adhere to the edict she had been given. At the same time she felt the need to remind herself of her own authoritative role although she did attempt to create a level of emotional safety for herself by attempting to remain neutral and calm. Judy sought to disassociate her authority and compassion by trying to control her own feelings and emotions. This incident further illustrates some of the dilemmas that confront women in leadership – ethically, professionally, politically and personally. Judy did not feel comfortable with the decision but was required to exercise her power and authority to get staff 'buy-in'. She was denied the opportunity to question the proposals herself and was charged with responsibility for relaying the message to staff. It appears from the transcript that although Judy was in a powerful position (as a dean), she was powerless in this situation. There was a message that had to be delivered to staff.

In her senior role Judy was required to perform, irrespective of the levels of discomfort this induced. Debra, one of the attendees at that meeting recalled:

> Change goes on here all the time. We are constantly told that the only certainty is change. I remember when the changes to the faculty were first mooted. Judy our Dean called a meeting. We all knew she was delivering a message and that message could not be good. She seemed at first very calm and very careful to outline what the proposed changes would be. The staff was angry, a few harsh words were flung around. Judy looked like she wanted to cry but she held it together. She tried to acknowledge our feelings but when she kept getting the same old people saying the same old hurtful things, she reacted. We have never really heard her be angry but she was. The room went silent. No one spoke after that.

Although Judy was herself emotional about what was to occur with the faculty restructure, the expectation was that she would manage staff reaction and get their 'buy-in'. The personal cost in this situation was high: stress, disillusionment, disappointment and a painful incident for both Judy and the staff. She had been placed in an untenable situation as a buffer between the staff and the DVC. She was responsible for 'delivering a message' (Debra) that had originated at another level in the university. Judy had to manage herself and her emotions and be seen to manage the negative reaction of staff. Ultimately her struggle was with herself as an individual and herself as a person with power. Staff expected Judy to manage her inner professional self (keep calm, keep emotions in check) and at the same time manage her organizational self (deliver the message). In this incident the collective impacts of power, authority, leadership and gender were unpredictable and uneasy (Acker 2012).

Conclusion

As this chapter has highlighted, women use terms such as 'rules' and 'game' to highlight their perceptions of the institutional culture and what it means to be in a management role in an institutionalized environment such as a university. Ostensibly the game that was referred to was the dominant system of knowledge, beliefs and practices that dictated the 'fit' with the prevailing institutional culture. Decisions to opt in and play the game, reject the rules, or opt out are seldom straightforward. To comply involved a level of complicity with the rules (Swan and Fox 2010; Thomas and Davies 2002) or rejecting these rules and remaining on the outside (Deem and Ozga 2000). The rules are seldom devised by women but they must learn them in order to survive in academia. Nor do women participate in the game on an equal footing and consequently, from the outset, they are travellers in a male world.

I have shown in this chapter the dynamics and dilemmas women leaders face in the privileged and gendered social order within management. Interactions between women may not always be positive and self-affirming and differences in perceptions can be exaggerated as a way of preventing change that ultimately destabilizes the 'natural' order. Rather than being accepted or celebrated for moving into senior roles, women leaders are punished for violating scripts about desirable femininity (Halvorsen 2002; Priola 2007).

What these stories tell us is that women's participation at senior levels frequently occurs on an oppositional basis. That is, they experienced alienation in committee rooms and in meetings, the processes favoured their male colleagues, and resistance appeared to be futile. Although each of the women reported attempts to change the status quo, they were ultimately caught in a paradoxical situation in which resistance produced a level of condescension and discrimination.

Chapter 5

Dangerous terrain?

Women leaders are caught in a tangled web as they mediate and negotiate their own roles and institutional authority. Both their male and female colleagues carry contradictory expectations about how women ought to lead and manage. This chapter traverses dangerous terrain as I expose ways in which women leaders do not act in positive and self-affirming ways. This chapter looks beyond blaming women as the problem but asks more serious questions about the problems of leadership and whether the complexities of women's lives as leaders can be fully understood. Drawing out these complexities, I narrate the experiences of Indigenous women and the dangerous terrain they occupy.

Introduction

Metaphors such as the glass ceiling (Kanter 1993), glass escalator (Williams 1992) and glass cliff (Ryan *et al.* 2007) have been used to explain various barriers women face, male ascendancy in the workplace and the precarious position that those women who do succeed can occupy. These metaphors, as well as more recently introduced images such as concrete walls, leaky pipeline, chilly climate and boys' club reinforce institutional norms that frame leadership as male territory. These are no less than metaphors of entrapment that unproblematically characterize women as victims of the circumstances in which they find themselves. This narrow set of reductive metaphors does not acknowledge the degree of agency women do have or recognize that some women do thrive in the managerialist climate of higher education (Fitzgerald 2012b).

In many ways, women appointed to senior positions are transgressors. They dare to venture into this male and masculine territory and their very presence is a challenge to the organizational status quo (Saunderson 2002). From the outset women leaders and managers can encounter organizations that undertake 'remedial' work to address ambiguities created when women become occupants in a male world (Gherardi 1996). This remedial work includes individual and collective strategies undertaken by both women and men to restore a level of (gender) order that has been disrupted by women stepping out of and away from their traditional or perceived conventional roles. Part of this remedial work may involve women adopting tough and masculine management approaches, trying to blend in as 'one of the boys' while simultaneously being given the message that they are subordinate and inferior. Women occupy dangerous, unfamiliar and risky terrain in the organizational hierarchy.

The presence of women in senior roles in an organization can be deeply threatening. Women can, for example, expose what is missing from an organization such as the ethic of caring, attention to equity and diversity and collaborative ways of working and, furthermore, can interrupt prevailing policies and practices by placing gender on the management agenda (Acker 2012). Not only then are senior women potentially threatening to the organizational status quo; they occupy dangerous terrain precisely because of their gender. Responses to this threat are varied; women are simply ignored, excluded, regarded as 'lightweight' by their male colleagues, or dismissed as less than competent. In her recollection of the appointment of a woman to a senior role, Marion (SL) recounted that:

> They [senior management] didn't want to appoint another senior woman. Two women had applied and three men. Well [he] was arguing that [the preferred candidate] would be incompetent, but the other side of that is that she is seen as a difficult woman. So what they were thinking I guess was, do you appoint the one who can do the dishes or the annoying one who won't do the dishes?

This type of response is symptomatic of historical and cavernous organizational problems as well as the debilitating and exclusionist male culture that exists in management (Sinclair 1998). The myriad inequalities that women face have their origins in repeated patterns of gendered disadvantage that permeate institutional cultures.

Less talked about are those women who do not necessarily act in affirming ways and who may deter their female colleagues from considering leadership roles. Just as difficult is the conversation about female colleagues who do not support women leaders and who cast them as 'other' precisely because they either act like 'one of the boys' or seek to 'mother' their peers (Bendl 2008; Prichard and Deem 1999). Stung by this rejection by their female colleagues, the leader can ignore the situation, be weighed down by the burden of expectations or develop a corrosive leadership as a way to cope with relentless criticism. Positioned as an intruder by her male colleagues and as 'other' by her female colleagues, the woman leader is both isolated and constrained by existing structures.

Women leaders are caught in a tangled web as they mediate and negotiate their own roles and institutional authority. Both their male and female colleagues carry contradictory expectations about how women ought to lead and manage (Gherardi and Poggio 2007). Hence, the 'woman leader' is fixed in the institutional spotlight and her performance as a leader is constantly scrutinized.

There are two equally unappealing options; manage like a man (Bryans and Mavin 2003; Collinson and Hearn 1996), or respond to gendered expectations and manage like a mother (Due Billing and Alvesson 2000). Beyond this typology lies a level of risk and blame. In the first instance, women risk a level of condemnation as they do not conform to preconceived ideas about 'women leaders'. Equally, women who play the organizational game and link their work more closely with the performative demands of the institution can be labelled queen bees, ice queens or bullies. There appears to be no retreat from scrutiny and criticism as senior women struggle to be recognized for their talents and abilities while at the same time their female colleagues carry expectations that they will represent the interest of all women. Kanter (1993) has pointed out that when women constitute the minority in male cultures, in order to avoid isolation they become members of the dominant group; a membership that is seldom welcomed by either their female or male peers.

In this chapter I consider women's relationships with other women. Discussing negative interactions between women leaders and their colleagues is dangerous terrain as it potentially 'blames' women for being unable to cope with institutional demands. While negative behaviours between men can be overlooked and dismissed as 'competitive', negative behaviours (Miner and Longino 1987) by or among women perpetuate beliefs that women are ineffectual leaders. As I will show, women who submit to or accept the gendered structures and order, perhaps unknowingly, reinforce a gendered status quo. I do recognize that women do not always act in self-affirming ways (Gini 2001). The 'management as male' mantra (Haslam and Ryan 2008; Schein and Davidson 1993) socially constructs and impacts on women's behaviour towards women in senior management. Senior women can provoke powerful anxieties and ambivalences in their female and male colleagues.

Think crisis, think female

The work of Haslam and Ryan (2008) has revealed that in times of crisis, it is more likely that women will be appointed to senior positions. Explanations range from those that are relatively benign, such as the need for organizational change, to those that malign, such as inferences that decisions were made due to friendships, to those that point to the availability of opportunity due to reorganization or previous resignations. Obvious requirements for any manager during a time of crisis would include the ability to change things around, manage staff through the crisis and take an active role with stakeholders, community and the wider public (Ryan and Haslam 2005). These are the traits usually associated with women leaders (Eagly and Carli 2007). If women are not able to produce the necessary outcomes, poor performance can be attributed to individuals not the institution itself. Rather than drawing attention to their hazardous position, women are more likely to downplay the significance of the glass cliff to avoid being cast in the role of victim or attract the attention and criticism of those in power (Ryan and Haslam 2005; Ryan *et al.* 2007). Being in a numerical minority, women are under intense pressure not to fail – as men and sometimes their female colleagues wait for them to do so (Eggins 1997). Amanda (academic) observed the precarious nature of one senior woman's appointment:

> Jill was appointed to a portfolio that did not previously exist. No advertisement, so I was surprised when her appointment was announced. We were told she was very capable, we were told about all the other changes she'd done in other places.... It was pretty impressive.... But then I realized it was a poisoned chalice. She walked into it. There was a round of bargaining going on, unions were unhappy, staff thought management was out to get them, to get them to work harder for even less, and Jill was supposed to get a new workload system in place. We were told she would sort it all out, get agreement, get a workable system. Well she became the symbol for all that went wrong. No one was happy. And you know it didn't work, no one was happy, no one understood what it was all about. Compliance with the new system and ... towards the end we were told a consultant would be coming in to review the system ... and next thing you know Jill was gone.... It's still talked about as the system Jill built. I hadn't thought about that before. Jill built it, Jack wasn't happy, Jill fell down. Well that just about says it all.

The perception here is that Jill failed to devise a uniform workload system that could be implemented across the university. During a fractious time in the ebb and flow of university life (workplace bargaining, unhappy staff), Jill was appointed to secure agreement about how teaching, research and service work should be allocated to academics. There is a hint in Amanda's account that Jill's career trajectory suited her well for this role. The suggestion is that the job was a 'poisoned chalice' and that Jill had been put in a risky position. Intriguingly, Amanda mentions that Jack (presumably a reference to the male VC who instigated the process) was not satisfied with the outcome. At this point Jill became expendable, the scapegoat for the crisis. This left her open to criticism by peers and colleagues who 'still talk about the old system'. Jill was disproportionately blamed for the negative outcomes; there was little or no recognition of the circumstances surrounding this process of institutional change.

In this situation, there appeared to be no hesitation in putting a woman in an unpredictable and potentially stressful situation. This resonates with the work of Ryan *et al.* (2007) and Haslam and Ryan (2008) that has shown in times of crisis the mantra is not 'think manager, think male', but 'think crisis, think female'. The complex dynamic is that as more women move into senior roles, discriminatory actions such as appointing them to portfolios that carry a high degree of risk reduce the possibility of success. Yet again the dominant group is able to heighten the boundaries and protect their own interests.

Haslam and Ryan (2008) have shown that precarious positions provide opportunities for women to move into senior roles. As Sheryl (SL) recalled:

> My previous job had been advertised at least twice that I recall. One of my colleagues at another university encouraged me to apply. I was a bit hesitant because I had heard it was one of those jobs no one really wanted. Just think, quality, university, audit and you can almost hear the sighs. But I thought, why not? So I applied, got the job and yeah, it was tough. It was one of those jobs that is never finished and no one is ever satisfied with the results. 'Could do better' is what any quality audit says. But I had a great team around me, we worked well and that role then opened up other opportunities. I guess I got known for being able to build a team, work across an institution and shift thinking about the value of audits. So having a job no one really wanted turned into me getting the job I have now, the job I want.

In some instances, women were simply not prepared to continue working in an environment in which they felt disconnected and disempowered:

> After a while it was all too much. I have a great life out of work, I'm at the time in my life when I can choose to work or choose to retire. I don't want to play this game any longer. I don't want to keep justifying myself. This is not me. There are better things for me to be doing, things for me and that's what I am going to choose. This is not my game any more.
>
> (Kayla, SL)

It would seem that Kayla no longer wanted to be seduced by the leadership and chose to exit the institution. Similarly Colleen (SL) raised the following question:

> Is it better to fight that battle even if you lose, or is it easier at the end of the day to just not fight the battle and let the status quo continue or should I just leave? At the end of the day, the last option is looking more and more appealing. It's looking like the only option and I'm not sure that it should be the only option.

For Kayla being able to walk away from 'this game' was powerful. She was able to make the choice to remain or walk away. Walking away for her was a rejection of the game, a form of localized tactics to regain 'a great life out of work'. Colleen saw leaving as a less than desirable option but necessary as she did not wish to continue to 'fight the battle'. Confident of her own place in the institution, Melissa expressed her view that 'they [senior management] are not going to sack me. They can't. They need me more than I need them. I've got enough money now to retire.' Neither Kayla nor Melissa wished to be damaged by the institutional culture in which they worked and were able to exercise their choice to leave the academy. But what each of these examples shows is that none of the women was able to shift the masculine culture.

Boundary breaking and boundary heightening

Kanter's (1993) work on the sociology of gender explores the dynamics of corporate behaviour and the problems groups in the numerical minority face. Newcomers who join an established and homogeneous group, and who are different in terms of culture, gender or ethnicity, offer a particular challenge to that group. Visible, as they are not immediately camouflaged by the sameness of the group, newcomers are constantly scrutinized to see if they 'fit' with the group and the organization. Kanter (1993) terms this 'boundary heightening' that is designed to test newcomers, gauge their resilience as well as their willingness to conform and fit in. Newcomers who are not compliant risk being isolated. A number of women remarked on these behaviours:

> I recall my first senior management meeting. Yeah, how scary was that. I introduced myself but all I got back was 'who do you barrack for?' I had no idea what this meant and so I could only stare back. How was I to know it was a football team they were asking me about? Anyway, I do remember that someone in the room offered a name, can't remember what it was, but then the others all laughed. I think whatever was called out was a derogatory name for the team and that this was supposed to be my team. I just hate Monday and Friday meetings. Monday is all about the footy, Friday is all about tipping. I think that's a football term but I don't want to ask.
>
> (Sheryl, SL)

> The university sponsored some game or maybe it was a team. There was publicity on email and on the intranet. International students were given tickets to go and a bus was put on. The VC, senior management team and some members on Council went. I was not asked along, I was not given a ticket. When I asked about this I was told 'we thought you wouldn't be interested'. Well I wasn't, I don't like sport, it doesn't interest me, but that's not the point. I was not even invited and it was just the boys' club that went along. The next week all they seemed to do was talk about the event and I could not join in this conversation either.
>
> (Jackie, SL)

In both examples Sheryl and Jackie are estranged from the group because they do not understand (or want to understand) sports talk. This is a form of gender demarcation that Kerfoot and Knights (2004) argue works to isolate women and reinforce masculinity as the organizational norm. Indigenous women are doubly isolated based on their gender as well as their ethnicity. As Myra reported:

> It's like double jeopardy. It starts with those damn adverts. You know the ones that encourage women and minorities to apply. I feel like I have to decide if I'm one or the other. But in a White place I can't identify with White men or White women. But I'm expected to. Which has the capital – White or women? It just sets me apart from the get go.

A recurring theme in the literature on feminist management in higher education is the continual tension between feminist ideals and the contradictory demands of the corporatized university (see for example Fitzgerald and Wilkinson 2010; Keller and Moglen 1987; Morley 1999). Feminist leadership is risky work as it ultimately poses a direct challenge to the organizational status quo. Feminist women have the capacity to rupture taken-for-granted assumptions and practices and can provoke a backlash as individuals seek to reinforce institutional norms (Gherardi and Poggio 2007). Working to dismantle these norms can unsettle the majority men as Heather (SL) revealed:

> I readily tell women that I am a feminist but I don't have to name myself as they all know. When I say this out loud in a mixed group it makes them as nervous as hell. It seems to close down the conversation. I don't play by the rules and this makes some men suspicious, maybe even uncomfortable. They never seem to know what I will say, they think I have an agenda.

In this example, Heather's willingness to name and make visible her feminism was not viewed favourably 'in a mixed group'. Presumably the reaction to disengage with her, 'close down the conversation', came from colleagues uncomfortable with her position and positioning. The silences this provoked were a form of disapproval for the agenda Heather appeared to be promoting (Hatcher 2003; Knights and Kerfoot 2004). Ultimately Heather had transgressed as she had failed to follow the rules by confronting the imposed order. The impact of her naming her practices and commitment as a feminist was perceived as a form of intimidation, hence the suspicion and unwillingness to continue a conversation. The institutional rules evident here suggest that women should not mobilize their feminist selves but should work to avoid conflict and enact different patterns of action in order to fit in with the dominant group (Gherardi and Poggio 2007; Mavin and Grandy 2012).

Feminist women can evoke powerful reactions from their colleagues. Feminist women have a commitment to social justice and social change that involves an explicit attempt to challenge the unequal distribution of power, hierarchical structures and discriminatory practices (Hughes 2000; Wyn *et al.* 2000). Feminist management is equated by some with flattened organizational structures, and for many with consultative, participatory and collaborative ways of working

(Acker 2012; Blackmore 1999; Deem and Ozga 2000) that create more inclusive and more caring ways of leading. This is exemplified by Lorna (academic) who observed:

> There's a lot of talk about being consultative, being collaborative, being inclusive. This is what feminists are about. It's a good way to work because it brings people along with you. I think it's about how you work with people, how you treat people. It shouldn't be about labels.

Being a feminist in the academy presents women with equally unattractive options. Particularly at senior levels there are concomitant institutional expectations and obligations that may not sit easily with feminist principles, values and ways of working. As Donna (SL) observed: 'I am a feminist but the more I progress in my career the more I am driven by a desire to succeed. I no longer feel connected with my colleagues.' In this situation the competitive, individualistic and single-minded culture of the university created a division between Donna and her colleagues. She found herself continually having to make decisions about the 'rules to follow and the rules to challenge'. Donna later indicated that she 'struggle[s] with the expectations, demands and obligations' placed on her; the performativity demanded generated an uncomfortable tension with her feminist principles. This incongruence rendered management 'an uncomfortable space' (Donna) that ultimately places 'woman' and 'leader' in tension, as well as 'feminist' and 'leader' (Mauthner and Edwards 2010). What appears to have occurred was that as Donna moved into a senior role the greater was the pressure for her to conform to the institutional culture (Meyerson and Scully 1995).

Women who identified with feminism were subject to a particular backlash from their female colleagues:

> The only negative behaviour in the women I've worked under or observed at first hand that I can comment on is that I'm personally not a feminist and I have difficulty with people who have a feminist paradigm and operate under a feminist paradigm in their leadership. To my mind and from my experience feminists are out to prove they are better than males and I can't identify with that. What I might be picking up is something that is not part of a strict definition of feminism but it is a behaviour that I see that goes along with people who call themselves feminists. Those aggressive behaviours replicate the whole male thing.
>
> (Noelle, SL)

Lynette, a feminist leader, struggled with her own decision to apply for a senior role. 'Sooner or later,' she said, 'I'll find myself acting like a man' because 'sometimes it's the only way to fit it, to get things done'. For Lynette becoming a DVC offered opportunity to 'support women in this place and get some change happening for women', but she was painfully aware that she would need to 'blend in, not rock the boat' because 'after all a five-year contract comes up for renewal pretty quickly'. Similarly, Morley (1999) has highlighted the dissatisfaction senior women managers experience as they attempt to cope with hierarchical and bureaucratic structures and adhere to their feminist principles. Lynette admitted that:

> Leadership posed lots of difficulties for me, lots of problems. As a feminist I wanted to be democratic in the way I went about my job. But I felt myself being autocratic. It was just easier, it got the job done. But when I held to my principles this seemed to be interpreted as being soft, not being direct enough.

Feminist women who are consultative, collaborative and egalitarian can be dismissed as lenient or indulgent primarily because they do conform to gendered expectations as the above extract shows. Feminist women who strive to change the cultural values in their university and contest the unrecognized and unacknowledged power and authority vested in their male colleagues occupy risky terrain (Bendl and Schmidt 2012). This is apparent in the recollections of Margaret (SL) who wanted to 'rock the boat. I can, I know I can. But I'd better not rock it too much that I get thrown out too. Can I rock it and stay in? Not sure.' In other words, Margaret wanted to agitate for change as well as remain an organizational insider (Meyerson 2001). Evident in Lynette's narrative is the desire to be a good-girl feminist (Gallop 1995) and to 'get the job done' by not being 'soft' but by being 'direct'. Margaret, on the other hand, displayed a level of bad-girl feminist as she worked to 'rock the boat' and agitate for change. This binary suggests that a level of corrective action is required. Being either a 'good girl' or a 'bad girl' are two equally unattractive options that places blame on women if their leadership is perceived as inadequate. Or is it the case that the hyper-visibility of women exposes them to increased surveillance, criticism and risk?

Kanter (1993) has described activities that invoke solidarity behaviour such as establishing a network of allies and forming alliances and coalitions. One immediate assumption of this solidarity behaviour is that it will invariably induce women to support and encourage one another. Secondly, there is an inherent assumption that women who do attain these senior positions are proactive role models for the female peers (Mavin and Bryans 2002; Mavin and Grandy 2012). A further assumption is that relationships between women are positive and affirming (Miner and Longino 1987) and that women ought to engage in behaviours which support and sponsor women's progress up the academic hierarchy. What appears to have been overlooked is that in moving to senior roles, women are moving away from their female colleagues. The majority of women in university management are located at the middle tier, as heads of school or heads of department. Moving up to senior manager as a dean, PVC, DVC or VC is a move to a rare, isolated and lonely place for women. Far from being sisters and part of a wider network, senior women are exiles from their sex (Wajcman 1998).

Implicit in the sisterhood and solidarity thesis is the unquestioned belief that women are 'natural' allies and that women ought to build alliances with one another. Men do not necessarily see each other as 'natural' allies; more likely they see each other as competitors. 'Individual women cannot be understood separately from the society, culture or context in which she works' (Fagenson 1993: 6). Those women who have reached senior levels have done so by out-performing men (Gini 2001). Consequently, they risk being labelled queen bees (Mavin 2006) as they encounter the uncomfortable and exclusionary terrain of senior management. It is at this senior management level that women are expected to work for and on behalf of their women colleagues and that sister-hood and solidarity will trump the masculinist environment. Condemnation can be quick and unequivocal. Megan (academic), for example, criticized a woman leader who was 'well known for climbing up the ladder and then once there, quickly pull[ing] up the ladder behind her'. In an environment where there is not a critical mass of women, those who are in senior roles are hyper-visible, hyper-scrutinized and, when possible, kept in their place.

In their place

Women are very much exiles in senior management (Marshall 1984; Wajcman 1998). Women at the top of the academic hierarchy are inevitably placed at a distance from their less senior women colleagues as well as in competition with one another. Sharon (SL) expressed her deep concern that 'senior women man-agers present a threat to each other at the top and because of their infighting and lack of support are too easily dismissed by male colleagues'.

The primary solution to the current inequities in senior leadership has been to rehabilitate statistics through placing more women in these roles. However, any attempt to see this as a problem of numbers without addressing inherent institutional gender bias perpetuates incongruities between being a 'manager' and being a 'woman'. Unhelpfully, women are expected to be able to compete with their male colleagues but be neither 'one of the boys', nor 'mother' their colleagues (Acker 2012); engage in solidarity behaviour; represent the interests of women; not 'blame or fix'; and be recognized for their talents and abilities. Simply put, women are expected to simultaneously play hard and play nice as the following example indicates:

> One [woman leader] was just really out for herself, taking opportunities and doing what she thought would make her look good. The other was com-pletely different and wanted to do what she thought would be best for the institution, wanting to fix things for people so that things could work smoothly and she could look good too.
>
> (Julia, academic)

Playing nice did not involve raising awareness of institutional imbalances. For example, in the words of Alison (SL), 'what I get when I mention a gender imbalance [in committees] is "not that again" and then I know if I continue I will be accused of being defensive'. Responses such as this worked as a powerful form of control to keep Alison in her place (Goode and Bagilhole 1998). Hence, Alison was vulnerable due to both her gender and her willingness to confront inequitable institutional structures and processes. And rather than examine whether the gender imbalances on committees are a systemic problem, institutions locate women such as Alison who raise the question as the problem. This is not to suggest that women wish to be mere bystanders or endorse what is occurring. Asking questions reveals awkward and persistent truths.

In many instances, women compete with their female peers for portfolios aligned with student services, quality and equity (Fitzgerald and Wilkinson 2010). This competition sets women in opposition to one another as well as at a distance from one another. Successful women may find themselves defending the institutional status quo in male-dominated organizations (Kanter 1993) or expected to align themselves with the masculinist culture in order to 'fit' (Connell 2006; Gherardi 1996). Much of the literature on women and leadership uncritically assumes sisterhood and solidarity among women leaders and their colleagues. Sisterhood and solidarity behaviour may in fact set expectations of senior women that cannot be fulfilled and open these women up to criticism and rebuke. A number of studies have shown that, compared with men, women can be less supportive of the careers of their female colleagues, question their commitment to the organization and be less supportive of equal opportunities programmes (Garcia-Retamero and Lopez-Zafra 2006; Ng and Chiu 2001; Noble and Moore 2006).

The metaphor of the queen bee (Mavin 2006) has been used to describe women who have been individually successful in a male-dominated environment. This may well be a characterization based on an inherent hostility or envy directed towards women in senior positions. These women have not shown solidarity with their female colleagues and they are perceived as having moved away into a senior role. The cumulative effect is that senior women are positioned as 'other' to their female colleagues; they are other women who now do not belong to this group. Rather than recognize their achievements, rhetorical devices such as 'queen bee', 'wannabees' (Mavin 2008) and 'ice queen' are used to reduce their legitimacy as leaders. Additionally, the queen bee label is attached to women who are perceived to be gatekeepers as they do not create pathways for their female colleagues:

> There was this terrible woman professor here when I first arrived who when I was interviewed for the job proudly said 'you're the first woman we have interviewed for a job since I've been here'. She was one those women who had got to a position and kept other women out. Bit like a queen bee really.
>
> (Debra, academic)

Queen bees set themselves apart from their female colleagues by emphasizing their masculine characteristics (such as independence, dominance) and stressing their differences to other women (Derks *et al.* 2011). Women who undermine other women by repeating stereotypical assertions are less likely to be interpreted as having a gender bias or being sexist as they are repeating, reinforcing and thereby legitimizing the gendered status quo. Stereotypical opinions expressed by women are not just detrimental but perceived as credible and persuasive precisely because women have uttered the sentiments. Paula (academic) recalled:

> I went along to a seminar once. A number of senior staff, all women, they were invited to talk about their career, the challenges they faced, you know, that sort of thing. I asked a question about how they coped with having young children, doing a PhD and getting a career on track. I remember one Dean who was there saying something like 'oh, you just get on and do it. You can. I did. Don't make children an excuse.' I felt dismissed, that I was a failure because I was struggling to cope.

Margaret (SL) spoke of her anger about a women colleague in a previous institution who:

> constantly tried to be 'one of the boys'. She used to brag that she could drink the boys under the table. But it was not just that. She also told sexist jokes. I think she was trying to be one of the boys. But I was horrified to hear her belittle a recently appointed woman. Her view was that X had got the job because she would 'look good in the senior management photo'.

If women perceive their gender to be a liability, this may induce them to advance their career through queen bee behaviour. Hence, queen bees have the capacity to 'sting' particularly when their powers are threatened (Mavin 2006). They fear the success of women colleagues who may, in turn, challenge their own position in the institutional hierarchy (Kanter 1993). Debra, a senior lecturer, reported:

> Once I began to question her it was like a switch had been turned on, and whenever you employ someone in a sessional way or in a RA [research assistant] way, on contract or project at my previous university the attitude was pretty clear that there are plenty more where they came from. And I think that applies in the sector actually. It was the mentality of this particular woman. I'd heard that she operated that way. I'd heard from people at her former university. She had a professor behind her, she wasn't at that level, and she was his head kicker. So in a way she had learned to work this way.

This account speaks to the difficult position women leaders frequently encounter as they attempt to act like a male (a 'head kicker') and learn to 'work this way', while at the same time exercising a level of abusive leadership. Debra was powerless to confront this behaviour as she relied on being employed on further research contracts. The sting that Debra felt was that the woman was using her own position to promote her career while at the same time marginalizing the team member (Reay 2000).

The queen bee label has been offered as evidence that women are their own worst enemies and that rivalry among women is an obstacle to career advancement (Mavin 2006; McCarthy 2004). Megan's (academic) view is illustrative of this point:

> I was invited to apply for a job by this woman. I wasn't going to apply for the job because I didn't want it, but I thought if this woman who I knew didn't like me had told me to apply for the job maybe I should apply for the job. So I applied for the job. I was never going to get the job. I don't even know why I did, but I thought maybe I would get it.... She'd tried to say yes you are a very valuable colleague. She flattered me and then of course she didn't give me the job. She was on the selection committee and I found out there was no chance that I was ever going to get the job because I would have had to work too closely with her and she didn't want to work with me.

Although the metaphor of the queen bee may be useful in understanding the negative impact exerted by women, ultimately, women are blamed for their own and other women's unequal career opportunities and outcomes. Kanter's (1993) study has shown that any female or male worker with less power and less opportunity, found in scarce numbers at any organizational layer, would be perceived by their colleagues in similar ways. Notably, there is not an equivalent queen bee label or metaphor to describe men who do not behave well towards their peers. Indeed, poor behaviour from men in senior management can be deemed competitive and is rendered acceptable. Men in senior roles are neither expected to support their women colleagues nor condemned when they fail to do so.

Continued use of labels such as queen bee pejoratively constructs women as unsuitable for senior management and legitimizes why it is wrong for women to occupy senior positions (Mavin 2008). Assumptions that women form alliances and support one another create a binary view of women. Women actively working for and on behalf of their women colleagues are labelled 'good', whereas women who appear to have abandoned women's interests are labelled 'bad'. In effect, at both edges of the binary women are blamed if they are unable to make an impact or if they continue to be more male than men (Bryans and Mavin 2003; Mavin 2008). But women can work against their female colleagues as Lynette (SL) points out:

It was female leadership at a very senior level of a university; it was management by intimidation; it was management by raising the bar. You jump over
it and then the bar goes up to the next height and unfortunately, you know,
that was a woman leader who was knee-capping people, other women as
well but certainly men, to the point that people were off on stress, people
were unhappy, morale was terrible. So it was management by intimidation,
and unfortunately I think that often does happen if there is a woman with
that kind of a disposition. That can be really, really toxic.

What remains problematic here is that in order to survive inhospitable and gendered institutional cultures, women adapt by identifying with more masculine
ways of working thereby distancing themselves from their women colleagues.
For Indigenous women such as Myra, the additional layer that she confronted
was that 'I am constantly reminded this [the university] is a White place and
about White ways' and in order to 'play by their rules' she needed to learn
'White ways'. Coping with the burden of acting White as well as surviving in the
gendered institution was for Myra 'not my reality, my way of knowing, my way
of working'.

The continued use of the label queen bee is unhelpful as it is part of a wider
discourse of keeping women in second place in management and continuing the
divide between women in management and senior management (Mavin 2006;
Olssen 2000). Certainly as a negative term queen bee symbolizes that women
leaders are a hindrance in senior leadership roles. More insidiously, the use of
this term by women is antagonistic as it works to blame the 'woman leader'
while ignoring the complex gender systems that exist. Viewing these narratives
through an alternative lens does not construct women as queen bees but rather
offers a way to interrogate ways in which the gender order is embedded and
socially constructs everyday experiences for senior women.

There can be little doubt that women are in a tenuous position in organizations. As previously noted, in the managerialist environment of higher education
individualism and competition are highly valued (Fitzgerald *et al.* 2012). To
compete, women must be assertive. Yet by asserting themselves they depart
from gendered expectations of compliance and non-competitiveness and are
likely to be resented. Female colleagues may resent a strong woman leader
because she exposes their own weaknesses and vulnerabilities (Lewis 2000;
Wilson 2005) as the following comment from Jane (academic) shows:

people have to have their own motivation and drive. She appeared not to
see that she would be knocking that. She had a severe effect: people thinking about giving up. It's partly a style and it's partly this kind of critical
parent speaking to a child: 'you know I am right, and I will correct you.'
One of her students described her, she said 'I was educated by nuns and I
don't need another head nun.' It's a critical parent style, it's not only
women who do it.... But she thought I was too close to students ... [She]

sent me some wonderful emails which insinuated some very nasty, you know very insulting things about my professionalism.

Women who do succeed to senior levels may experience censure or be subject to backlash if perceived as unfeminine, domineering or aggressive (Kanter 1993). And this criticism may well come from their female colleagues. For example:

> She was a professor, but she wasn't an academic manager. I didn't take any notice of her. I kept out of her way. I didn't like her.... She was a bitch, and she was boring, and she talked about herself all the time. I didn't admire her work.
>
> (Leesa, academic)

Negative comments such as these act as a form of control to keep women 'in their place'. Women are relegated to being bitches or good girls. Rather than having a positive impact for their leadership, women are seen as responsible for the continuing problems, pressures and tensions. The label 'bitch' suggests that women need to be fixed, whereas the label 'good girl' implies that women ought to be blamed. Used by women to describe women leaders, these labels negatively impact on how women are viewed across the organizations. Women may well form and participate in networks and alliances, but there is no guarantee that they will support women leaders. Expectations of solidarity behaviour from women do not necessarily hold across institutional boundaries, or up, down and across hierarchical academic structures. Sisterhood and solidarity can work to reinforce levels of symbolic violence across and within institutions (Blackmore and Sachs 2007).

Less acknowledged in the educational leadership literature is that women do not always lead in self-affirming ways (Gini 2001). They are caught between being perceived as a 'good' woman and a 'good' manager. Hence, their negative behaviours are disproportionately detected because of their high visibility due to their numerically distorted presence and polarized perceptions about how women ought to dress, act and lead. Here again women are paradoxically constructed as 'good' or 'bad' and women's work as leaders is 'valued only in the most marginal sense' (Ely and Meyerson 2000: 109). Stepping into senior leadership roles requires a level of adaptation as well as assimilation. Yet, it is the 'habitat of the powerful' (Corsun and Costen 2001: 4) that defines the rules against a set of masculinist practices and priorities. This is not to suggest that the rules of the game are transparent, as Lynette (SL) indicated: 'it is very difficult to play a game if you don't know what the rules are.'

Successful women are more likely to have had to play hard, play rough and play tough in order to outperform men. Louise (SL), in the text below, has had to be resilient as she has progressed through the university in order to cope with the environment and demands:

I think what my story means is that any woman who rises even to the modest level I find myself at it's like surviving hell – you have to be really tough and determined, but also have a lot of luck. You know, one or the other won't do. It's chance and I'm not sure if it is a good thing or not but I can roll with the punches, although I am getting pretty close to my limit. I can defy the odds.

The stories presented do show that women can take on male behaviours in order to fit into their new roles. To reach this level women have had to confront a number of barriers and have an intense realization that they are in the numerical minority. Expectations that they adopt solidarity behaviours and take up issues for and on behalf of women in the institution are not realistic. While women may wish senior women to be strategic on issues affecting women, this is not a role valued by the institution and potentially places senior women in an awkward if not risky position. More hazardous is the term 'token feminist' that, if applied, further undermines women, their work and institutional presence. Even the threat of being labelled in this way can leave women feeling intensely uncomfortable.

Implicit assumptions in all of these stories are that women leaders should be proactive and visible, that they act as role models and mentors and raise the profile of women across the institution, and that entrée into management is via women's own networks. It is erroneous to assume that women are natural allies (Mavin 2006) or that they are responsible for all women across the institution. Again, these expectations position senior women as responsible for 'fixing' the institutional culture that excludes women, or blamed if change does not occur. Trying to 'fit in' with a senior leadership team as well as 'fit in' with all women in the institution is simply not possible. Studies by Bagilhole and White (2011), Acker (2012) and Morley (2013) indicate that women who take up these senior positions do want to make a difference and do want to lead their colleagues in positive and affirming ways.

Conclusion

Frequently in the numerical minority, women leaders are highly visible at senior levels. Women are expected to simultaneously act in feminine and masculine ways to demonstrate their rejection of masculinist leadership on the one hand and to show that they can be authoritative, entrepreneurial and competitive on the other. It is an impossible situation that opens women up to accusations from both their female and male colleagues who harbour preconceived notions about leaders and leadership.

Wajcman (1998) argues that women find it difficult to deal with their senior women colleagues because the strategies they are accustomed to using with men are inappropriate for women. This raises a number of questions: can we safely, without blaming individual women, explore the contradictions and discontinuities between the call for senior women to engage in solidarity behaviour whilst continuing to label them as queen bees? If management is seen to be the domain of men, how then can women advance from beyond second place?

It is not an easy situation to understand or unravel. Women who progress to senior management continue to be viewed and evaluated as women. In many instances the unconscious or conscious oppression of women by women can be as a result of successful women being seen as norm violators (Parks-Stamm *et al.* 2008) and their female colleagues wanting to distance themselves from this. Successful women can pose a threat to the self of other women (Parks-Stamm *et al.* 2008) and a critical reaction can be provoked. Accordingly, when senior women do not conform to preconceived assumptions and expectations both women and men vilify them. The backlash response is to label them as queen bees; a label that simultaneously requires women to 'fix' the problems and blames senior women when they do not. There is no comparable term or label for men.

A reason why women may react negatively to women leaders is an inherent belief that senior women will align themselves with their interests. Unrealistic expectations combined with an anticipation of solidarity further exacerbate these perceptions. Less recognized are the tensions and contradictions senior women face in their everyday roles. A great deal of their time is occupied learning to survive. The 'women in management' mantle attempts to discursively position women in a tenuous position; they are either token men or token women. What is needed is a different future for women in senior management.

Chapter 6

Whispers of change

In institutionalized spaces such as universities, initiating and sustaining change are notably difficult and problematic. Although visible masculinist practices and beliefs predetermine 'the way things are', securing change is not impossible. On the institutional margins and in the less visible spaces women can quietly mobilize, bide their time and move about seemingly unnoticed. It is in these spaces in between where the potential for change lies. This chapter draws together the various themes in this book and cements the view that women are not powerless. I present the possibility of thinking about leadership from an Indigenous perspective and provoke readers to imagine how leadership might be reframed.

Introduction

Universities are complex and exciting institutions with a vibrant scholarly community. A cursory glance at any university website will highlight the range and breadth of its academic and research programmes, its community outreach and the impact of its presence. Paradoxically, although many universities host research centres or institutes and acclaim the intellectual contribution of academics engaged in research in the areas of gender, work and organizations, they appear to turn a deaf ear and a blind eye to this work when examining the institution itself (Wilson 1996). The continuous underrepresentation of women at senior levels and the numerical dominance of men ought to be a clear and public signal that there is a serious and persistent problem to be confronted (Fitzgerald 2012b; Fitzgerald and Wilkinson 2010; Sinclair 1998; White 2003).

For a woman to navigate to a senior leadership role, she must demonstrate that she possesses credible leadership skills, knowledge and dispositions. Immediately problematic is that these skills, knowledge and dispositions are linked with masculinity and men (Collinson and Hearn 1996; Wajcman 1998). Women who do display masculine behaviours do not 'fit' into prevailing stereotypes; that is, they do not conform to expectations held by either men or women. Women who do conform to feminine stereotypes display non-leadership behaviours that render the management layer more difficult to shatter (Mavin 2008).

The enduring mantra 'think-manager-think-male' (Schein and Davidson 1993) is highly problematic in universities in the twenty-first century. It implies congruence between people and their jobs and that those women who challenge the established gender order and stray onto the playgrounds of male power ought to be deterred. Women can either behave like women, thereby accentuating their institutional 'otherness', or seek to comply with masculine norms, thereby provoking a level of peer disapproval because they are seen as women trying to act like men (Itzen and Newman 1995; Schein 2007). The risk here is that if women surrender to these norms they are positioned as conciliatory and submissive (Due Billing 2011).

If the managerial habitus (Blackmore and Sachs 2007) is indeed male, then women might well be ambivalent about taking up leadership roles as they are inevitably faced with resistance because they do not fit established stereotypes; they are neither likeable nor nice. As relative newcomers to senior management, the tendency is to 'fit in' and adapt to the prevailing culture (Gherardi 1996; Wajcman 1998). Hence, to be successful, women need to demonstrate masculinity and suppress femininity. But to be accepted, they need to conform to established stereotypes and stay out of powerful positions. Whatever way these dilemmas are viewed, they create contradictions and ambivalences for women and produce normative femininities that still locate women as the institutional 'other' (Gherardi and Poggio 2007).

A further suggestion is that, once in senior roles, women act contrary to normative expectations and display their own managerial habitus. Women who accept these roles can be seen as 'good girls' or 'good girl feminists' (Gallop 1995). In the eyes of her female colleagues, the 'bad' girl is the one who seemingly rejects femininity and does not work to foster women. Alternatively, the 'bad girls' who adopt masculinities can be labelled 'queen bees', a derogatory term used to signal an overall displeasure or dislike of women in authority, and a term that has no male equivalent. There is evidence that cultural associations of power and authority with masculinity make it difficult for women to hold positions of power because of the contradiction between their gender identity and the masculinity of power (Charles and Davies 2000). Simply counting more women in by increasing their numbers across the academic hierarchy is not necessarily the antidote.

Although the 'male manager' is the institutional norm in the majority of universities, this managerial cage can be rattled. The first step then is to dismantle the 'think-manager-think-male' mantra and to interrogate more closely hegemonic discourses of the male norm (Due Billing 2011; West and Zimmerman 1987). This will require significant recognition of and attention to systemic gendered leadership expectations and the gendering of identities in universities. That is, universities are complicit in continuing patterns of structural discrimination as well as that institutionalization of 'traditional and narrow constructions of acceptable masculinities [in leadership and management] that have become a prison for both women and men' (Sinclair 1998:

57). The second step is to uncover the hidden curriculum of higher education that promotes the use of competitive self-promotion, the careful selection of leadership tasks and responsibilities, high visibility in decision-making committees, an unrelenting commitment to the institution and access to extensive networks of power, sponsorship and influence. Interwoven in this hidden curriculum are the 'rules of the game' that work to privilege a particular set of leadership dispositions (Blackmore and Sachs 2007; Morley 2013) and frame leadership as male territory. What is now required is new thinking about women's leadership that moves away from labels and metaphors and which frames leadership in more democratic, inclusive and socially just ways (Blackmore and Sachs 2007).

In essence, 'management incorporates a male standard that positions women out of place' (Wajcman 1998: 2). Accordingly, women are caught between dominant masculinist images and constructs of leadership and the realities of how the work is actually accomplished. Moving into a leadership role can mean some past practices need to be discarded and new practices and new priorities adopted. In re-presenting themselves, many women are caught between discursive binaries that position them as being both in and out of control.

This book has exposed a hidden dimension of leadership – female colleagues' perceptions of women leaders. These perspectives have been important to understand how 'leadership is constructed in the minds of the audience' (Sinclair and Wilson 2002: 176) as well as in the minds of senior women themselves. In many ways gendered perceptions about what makes a 'good' or 'bad' women leader work against women in uncompromising ways. That is, from their male colleagues point of view, 'good' women leaders are those who are seen to play the management game, yet they are rendered ineffective precisely because this game is not defined on their terms. From the view of their female colleagues, a 'good' woman leader works for and on behalf of her female colleagues. Being seen to be 'good' for this group inevitably means being labelled a 'bad' leader by her male colleagues as she has failed to demonstrate her commitment to upholding the institutional status quo. Ultimately, the 'bad' woman leader can be subjected to accusations of being a queen bee (Mavin 2006), as she fails to trumpet women's interests. Yet her male colleagues may label her a 'good' leader as she has not engaged in solidarity behaviour. These may well appear to be simplistic ways of presenting the problem, but what these binaries do signal is that the problem is one of both perception and structure. However the problem is then viewed, women cannot win as both her female and male colleagues wait for her to fail.

What this project has revealed is that women do not find leadership specifically problematic. Many women lead subject, curriculum and discipline teams, research projects and departments and schools. Women can and do succeed in these positions. However, once more formal management positions are taken up, women find these more problematic. Roles linked with an institutional title (such as dean, PVC, DVC) require a distance between women and their

colleagues and an immersion in an institutional culture that may be disconnected from the realities of women's lives. In many ways women are caught in
the institutional spotlight as they seek to co-operate with managerial demands
and expectations on the one hand, yet on the other, are conscious of the gendered demands of the workplace (Acker 2010).

Outsiders on the inside or insiders on the outside?

The ideal managerial worker in universities is one who is entrepreneurial and
productive, who is able to self-manage and self-regulate, is willing and able to
work long hours and demonstrates their commitment to the institution
(Blackmore *et al.* 2010; Fitzgerald *et al.* 2012). Management positions that
are coupled with male behaviours and characteristics (Collinson and Hearn
1996; Due Billing and Alvesson 2000) sustain an imagery of and association
with the male body. Consequently, women may be overburdened with tasks
and activities that are assumed to be 'natural' for women, and perhaps under-
burdened with others. This not only restricts ways in which women can lead
and manage but cements expectations about how women *ought* to lead and
manage (Acker 2012; Charles and Davies 2000; Fitzgerald 2012b; Mavin
2006; Sinclair 2004).

The choice for women can be to either play a gendered game (Acker 2010;
West and Zimmerman 1987) or resist the rules thereby exposing themselves to
sanctions for their deviance. Yet framing women as the victims of the male norm
is not a satisfactory answer. As the chapters in this book have shown, women's
everyday experiences in university management are complex, multifaceted and
complicated. There is a paradox at work here. Purportedly brought into an institution for their supposedly feminine skills, women are frequently placed in positions of being unable to utilize these skills as the institution demands the
inculcation of a different set of work practices associated with the masculinity of
management (Kerfoot and Knights 2004; Leonard 1998).

Devine *et al.* (2011) describe women as having an elastic self that demands a
care-less attention to performativity and completion while at the same time performing leadership against gendered expectations. However what is needed is
care-full attention to leadership and leading in order for more socially just practices to emerge.

Women leaders do have a degree of institutional power and authority ostensibly based on their position and portfolio in the academic hierarchy. As such,
they are insiders in the organizational bureaucracy and associated with the managerial career path. Certainly, as the numerical portrait depicts, women are the
visible minority in senior university management. They are the organizational
'other' and in order to succeed must manage this 'otherness' (Probert 2005;
Reay 2000). This does little to change the hyper-masculinity circulating around
management and renders university management trebly difficult, if not impossible, for Indigenous women who must negotiate their 'otherness' through

gendered and raced lines that situate all White men and White women, and Indigenous men in more dominant positions.

Predominantly located in institutional housekeeping roles, women are simultaneously part of the managerial fabric of the organization yet marginalized. On the basis of their gender they are outsiders to the masculinist culture that accentuates executive attributes (as opposed to scholarly attributes) such as tact, firmness, commitment, common sense, self-empowerment and assertiveness. Insider knowledge such as understanding the 'rules of the game' (Goode and Bagilhole 1998), knowing how to attract the attention of the VC, lobbying for support and being able to utilize the language and metaphors (usually associated with sport) that are inherent in the leadership game are essential. Playing the leadership game requires understanding of the dominant knowledge and beliefs that ascribe value to one set of practices and ignore or undervalue another. Any decision to opt into or out of the leadership game is not straightforward as there are perceived costs and advantages (Deem and Ozga 2000). As Joce (SL) pointed out, 'sometimes I need to play the game. I do it to survive really. But sometimes playing by the rules means I can get some traction on what's important.' But these rules are neither fixed, transparent nor gender neutral.

Despite a fundamental awareness that playing the leadership game was fraught, a number of participants spoke of the pleasure they derived when they knew what was going on and had a degree of agency:

> Yeah, it's a game. I know most of the rules now. So sometimes I set out to not play by the rules. It makes the blokes squirm, makes them uncomfortable. They can't deal with it. It's then my game and they don't know my rules ... you know they don't ask me the rules either. That would mean the blokes would have to admit there is a game in play.
>
> (Cecilia, SL)

Women who are able to play the leadership game are less likely to be strangers as the more senior they become in the organization, the more likely it is that they will demonstrate the kinds of masculine behaviour required (Miller 2006). Becoming more of an insider to this culture potentially renders a woman as an outsider to her female colleagues that can produce a clash of expectations and perceptions between the roles of 'woman' and 'leader'. Women are both outsiders on the inside and insiders on the outside. Being simultaneously positioned as outsiders and 'other' creates organizational space for women to exploit opportunities to be change agents, rather than themselves being exploited for their supposedly feminized skills and abilities (Blackmore 1996; Deem and Ozga 2000).

Being on the outside offers the possibility to agitate for change whereas being on the inside suggests a level of complicity with or acquiescence to the dominant culture. Or, as Eisenstein (1996) observed, women are caught between being mandarins or missionaries, elite and inaccessible bureaucrats or uncompromising in the pursuit of their agenda. Eisenstein's (1996) work suggests that women are responsible for either change (missionary) or the lack of progress (mandarin). Here again the spotlight is not turned on institutionalized gendered practices and how wider strategies of change can be enacted.

Although useful in terms of theorizing how women are located as the perennial outsiders, it might well be time to move beyond the framework of outsiders/insiders. Such discourses may reinforce the perceptions of the numerical invisibility of women as well as further inculcate gendered assumptions about leadership and management. The unhelpful aspect of the outside/inside thesis is that women are inevitably located on the periphery in these discourses while men are perceived as being 'naturally' at the institutional centre. Women are not passive recipients but they can be powerless to prevent stereotypical assumptions about what makes a 'good' or 'bad' woman leader (Acker and Feuerverger 1996).

Positioning women as 'outside' the organization suggests there is a desirable 'inside' location to which women seek admittance. Yet notions of outsider and insider, outside and inside, are inherently problematic primarily because they reinforce and reproduce the binary divisions. A notion of outside the institution holds out the promise that eventually entrance to the sacred grove may be secured (Aisenberg and Harrington 1988). This does little to challenge the nature of the institution itself or traditional patterns of work. Managerialist climates provoke a level of collusion, commitment and compliance with performative demands (Davies *et al.* 2006) without boundaries of time, space and emotion.

Contradictions and ambivalences

There is an unstated assumption that leadership, particularly at senior levels, can only be undertaken on a full-time basis. From an organizational viewpoint a relentless commitment to formal and non-formal work hours is an ongoing expectation (Doherty and Manfredi 2006). For women with responsibilities for home and family, any request or desire for a fractional appointment or more family-friendly work hours casts them as outsiders in greedy organizations. In this environment women are the organizational 'other' and must manage their 'otherness' or not succeed (Probert 2005). What is needed then is to unsettle assumptions that work and careers proceed on a full-time or part-time basis (Baruch and Hall 2004). The situation is more complex as women's work histories usually comprise periods of full- and part-time work. Despite the rhetoric of flexibility in the workplace, senior management remains a full-time domain. Women with so-called marketable skills in senior roles can negotiate a different set of conditions, usually linked with their retention in the organization or at a particular level.

In many ways women cannot win. They are confronted with simultaneous expectations of being managerial (read masculine) enough to be recognized as managers yet feminine enough to be recognized and acknowledged as women (Gherardi 1996). Crossing into a male-dominated environment can be equally confronting and uncomfortable for women. Some women cope with this by distancing themselves from their female colleagues as they attempt to balance being managerial and being female. Some women cope by distancing themselves from some aspects of the role and subsequently place themselves at risk of being accused of not being committed. Some women challenge, resist and reject universalizing discourses.

The adversarial nature of male norms such as controlling, competing, organizing, establishing rules and regulations and deferring to a higher authority (Wajcman 1998) are not immediately part of women's leadership toolkit. Women are more likely to apply relational, collaborative and participatory skills (Sinclair 1998). Women are criticized on the one hand for their supposedly feminine qualities that do not match the organizational male norm of assertiveness, competitiveness, task-orientation and traditional authoritarianism while, on the other, those who perform these managerial behaviours are reviled for being too masculine (Kloot 2004; Skelton 2005). Women do not benefit from acting in either feminine or masculinized ways in managerial jobs (Fagenson 1993), whereas men benefit from acting in both masculinized and feminine way in managerial jobs (Gherardi 1996). In a strong managerialist culture women who are perceived as feminine are at a disadvantage principally because their values and identities are not aligned with the dominant way of thinking 'manager' and 'management'. However, men who can demonstrate their caring and collaborative nature benefit from these 'new' styles of leadership (Deem and Ozga 2000).

There is an incongruity here because if women deploy aspects of femininity to make themselves more caring managers they are performing to expectations (Acker 2012; Due Billing and Alvesson 2000), but if they perform to the same expectations required of male leaders, they run the risk of being accused of adopting hegemonic masculine ways of leading (Fitzgerald 2012b). Conversely, male leaders who care are rewarded for their capacities to undertake such work (Blackmore and Sachs 2007; Connell 2006). Because masculinity is not equated with caring in the way that femininity is, men can practise care-less masculinity without sanction. Women cannot practise femininity in a care-less manner (Devine et al. 2011). Those that do are subject to criticism and rebuke. Women leaders have to practise gender in a managed way to retain their status as women and as managers (Acker 2010; Marshall 1984; Martin 2006).

Labels and metaphors serve to reinforce normalized expectations surrounding masculinized and feminized work. But it is too simple a solution to suggest that leadership should be demasculinized, or indeed, feminized. Work is divided along gender lines across public and private organizations and within and across professions. Repeatedly, the pattern is that the more high-status and valued the work, the more likely it is to be performed by men (Acker 1990) and reserved for certain clusters of (White) men and masculinities. What this also means is that men in the middle and bottom ranks perform undesirable work. Desirable work for women is, therefore, that which is performed at the middle and bottom of the institutional hierarchy. Extending this thinking further, the presence of women in high-status, high-value and high-reward positions, particularly in large numbers, is undesirable. A modest reshuffling can alter the gender order, but overall little seems to change. Less discussed is the extent to which women work to maintain this gendered order, either by dissuading and distracting female colleagues from management roles, or by colluding in discourses that seek to entrench masculine advantage.

Senior management jobs have been conventionally understood as difficult for women to obtain (Fitzgerald and Wilkinson 2010; Morley 2005b). Because of a presumed 'lack of fit', different strategies have been activated to rehabilitate these weaknesses. This has involved, for example, leadership development programmes for women (Sinclair 2004) or access to mentoring (Devos 2008; De Vries 2005) and women-only networks (Coleman 2011). These informal processes usefully assist with the kind of self-promotion necessary to gain senior roles, knowledge that men appear to access through male-dominated support systems (Collinson and Hearn 1996; Williams 1992) and sponsorship that enhances self-esteem, self-confidence and contact with career mentors. Despite the advantages of mentor programmes, the underlying emphasis is on aligning women with institutional norms and values; norms and values that do not necessarily reflect the needs, interests and aspirations of women (McKeen and Bujaki 2007). These programmes are often shaped according to perceived institutional and individual deficit and disadvantage. But structural inequalities remain intact and unexamined.

Morley (2005a) has argued that women's entry into senior management in universities may not necessarily serve women's collective and long-term interests. In a climate of new managerialism, the creation of roles that are specifically designed to advance managerial objectives (such as audit, accountability, quality assurance and performance management) and the successful securing of these positions by women may in fact signal that women are 'naturally' suited to institutional housekeeping roles. The level of conformity and demonstrated commitment to values such as self-reliance, efficiency, competition, merit and independence (Blackmore and Sachs 2007) reproduce rather than eradicate inequalities. In many ways women perform the toxic labour of management that requires adherence to performative regimes and practices. This is the poisoned chalice of organizational compliance that is borne by those who numerically have the least amount of power. In this climate women are constantly at risk as they carry the burden of transformation (Deem and Ozga 2000).

Sinclair (1998) has proposed a framework for thinking about the imbalance of women in management. What this framework illustrates is the cascading effect of the relative invisibility of women and the paralysing influence of gendered assumptions.

1 *Denial*: The numerical absence of women in senior management is not regarded as a problem.
2 *The problem is women*: Women do not have the necessary skills, abilities or dispositions to be managers and must learn and adopt masculine ways of working.
3 *Incremental adjustment*: The solution rests on targeted appointments of token women who already possess the necessary track record and are therefore not 'high risk'.
4 *Commitment to a new culture*: The exclusion of women is seen as evidence of deeper systemic problems that require new ways of thinking.

The implication is that organizations move from (1) to (4) as a way to create a more inclusive culture. Sinclair's model usefully suggests that the organization is the problem. This is an advance on thinking about women as the organizational problem who require intervention and improvement in order to solve the problem. Although a plausible model, a more nuanced understanding of exigencies of race, class and ethnicity would contribute to a meaningful revision. Certainly Sinclair's framework is helpful in thinking about how assumptions are institutionalized. Unhelpfully, this framework can develop a level of inertia unless an organization is willing to confront endemic problems. The potential of Sinclair's framework lies in the capacity to acknowledge the impact of gender and to make these issues visible. Yet the imbalance of women in management is a fundamental organizational problem and the commitment to a new organizational culture (step 4) is not possible unless inequities are challenged (Ely and Meyerson 2000).

A silence this project has uncovered is that the university itself is the problem. Worryingly, the academy's own claim to be the custodian and site of liberal ideas has failed in the arena of gender relations. The academy remains able to indisputably reproduce its own self-image as the critic and conscience of society. Morley (2001, 2013) has argued that the introduction of new neo-liberal practices, the rise of the sovereignty of the consumer and the repositioning of (higher) education as a product to be consumed and subject to consumer laws, have produced new understandings of organizational cultures and priorities. Attention has turned towards producing new workers for the global marketplace and higher education has become a commodity with measurable and public outputs. There are profound silences in regard to discourses of human rights, democracy and social justice, questions about equity and diversity within leadership and more collaborative and socially democratic ways of leading and managing. Thus, universities' organizational practices and values largely remain intact (Itzen and Newman 1995).

In institutionalized spaces such as universities, initiating and sustaining change are notably difficult and problematic precisely because of the persistence of gendered structures and processes that coterminously legitimize and ascribe neutrality to these processes. Institutional logics render visible masculinist practices and beliefs as 'the way things are' (Meyerson and Tompkins 2007: 308) and accordingly any change is difficult to secure. But it is not impossible. The ambivalences and contradictions that women experience can simultaneously disable and enable. But it is on the institutional margins and in the less visible spaces that women can quietly mobilize, bide their time and move about seemingly unnoticed. It is in the quiet spaces, the spaces in between, where the potential for change lies.

In the quiet spaces

Women are not powerless. Their power lies in their independence and the uncertainty that their presence creates (Marshall 1984). Certainly as Meyerson and Tompkins (2007) suggest, it is often in the marginalized spaces that support for change can be mobilized. Localized strategies can build momentum and can contribute to wider critical awareness of the need for change. The power of momentum does not necessarily rest with individuals but in the collective group. The risk that exists for those individual women who agitate for change is that they will be exposed, further marginalized, ignored or seen as a threat to the institutional status quo. This is the ultimate paradox women face – wanting to change the gendered status quo while at the same time maintaining a commitment to the institution. The more visible and the more senior a woman is in the institution, the greater the potential and pressure on her to effect change, and the greater the pressure to conform to institutional norms and practices.

Creating space for leadership is not always easy. Establishing or belonging to a supportive and trustworthy network of women leaders can lessen feelings of loneliness and isolation. Networks offer a mechanism for social exchange where reciprocity and trust can be built around informal relationships and professional obligations. Women-only networks and networking can provide a safe place and space for women to share experiences and build their own connections across a community of like-minded women. Although women in this project mentioned the number of formal and scholarly networks to which they belonged, few attended meetings or events due to travel distances, ongoing cost of membership or clashes with family responsibilities. Women did participate in ongoing informal networks that relied on a range of self-directed and self-selected activities such as meeting colleagues for coffee, seeking out colleagues in similar roles at other universities as well as email and teleconference contact with colleagues in overseas institutions. In Judy's (SL) view, 'the real value of networks' is that 'your colleagues keep you real' and that they 'give you strategies to deal with work, to deal with life'.

A study conducted by Henry and Pringle (1996) with Māori and non-Māori women-run organizations concluded that Māori women in leadership roles predominantly correlated their understanding and descriptions of their leadership practices within a Māori-centred framework. This framework moves beyond thinking about leadership by an individual to thinking about leadership as a set

Table 6.1

Term	Leadership
Kuia (elder grandmother)	Wise leader; authoritarian
Whaea (mother)	Guiding and leading from behind
Rangatira (tribal leader)	Autocratic and confident leader
Tohunga (expert)	Analytical and leading by expertise
Tuakana (eldest sibling)	Directive; leader-in-waiting
Wahine toa (warrior woman)	Leading by example and power of convictions
Teina (younger sibling)	Tentative; leading through friendship
Potiki (youngest sibling)	Daring; leading by force of personality
Tauiwi (foreigner)	Tentative leadership exhibiting a lack of confidence

Source: Henry and Pringle (1996).

of relational activities that is culturally responsive. As this framework indicates, *connection* in terms of their leadership identity is critical to understanding 'women' and 'leadership'. That is, circumstances of family, genealogy and connection with the land matter, particularly for Indigenous peoples.

What this Māori-centred framework illustrates is that leadership for/by Māori women is relational as well as generational; that is, as a female grows older and as her life experiences expand, she adopts different roles at different times. Here, leadership is derived from within the *whanau* (family) and *hapu* (tribal group) and related back to that structure. Becoming a leader and leading are conceptualized according to age, experience, skill and status. The respective role of a woman is valued. This framework suggests that a linear career that privileges credentials, networks and outcomes is simply not possible. Hence, affiliation, the connection between the individual, her past and her present determines how leadership is enacted. Bhabha (1994: 45) has argued that:

> The question of identification is never the affirmation of a pregiven identity, never a *self*-fulfilling prophecy – it is always the production of an image of identity and the transformation of the subject in assuming that image.

Broadly what is being suggested is that connections that are familial and linked with physical, spiritual and geographic space and place offer more embodied ways of looking at leaders and leadership. Connecting leadership with self and the identities that we carry merges past, present and future, histories and memories. It is not about self-importance, self-reference or perfecting self.

Leadership, whether formal or informal, is a responsibility that is bestowed on Indigenous women. There is a clear mandate to provide direction, generate change, and create the conditions for success (Battiste 2000). Crucially, leadership occurs within a framework of identity and culture that emphasizes connectedness and generational survival (Collins 1991; hooks 1989).

Despite the emergence of studies that contest the primacy of Western models of knowing and leading (Blackmore 2010; Essed 2000; Fee and Russell 2007), the underpinning assumption is that Indigenous leaders can and should acquire the same knowledge skills and abilities as their White colleagues. Not only is this aligned with 'one size fits all' compensatory approaches, debates about diversity and distinctiveness *between* and *among* women that simultaneously question ways in which Whiteness is constructed and positioned are absent.

One of the more invisible aspects of the academy and academic work is the exercise of White privilege that is threaded through the institution and individuals (Blackmore 2010). The Western male-dominated academy simultaneously marginalizes women academics yet provides a level of cultural privilege and advantage based on Whiteness (Fitzgerald 2010; Lucashenko 1994). Dominant White cultures remain the silent and unexamined norm. Indigenous women exist in a bicultural world (such as Aotearoa New Zealand) yet have to shape their careers in a Pākehā or White world while maintaining close connections with *whanau* (family) and *iwi* (people). They must learn to navigate between two cultural worlds (Fitzgerald 2010) as well as two gendered worlds of being female and being male. Indigenous women experience institutions in markedly different and complex ways from their Pākehā female colleagues. Hage (1994: 28) offers a possible explanation:

> The tolerated others are by definition within our 'sphere of influence'. They are part of our 'world' (society, nation, neighbourhood) but only insofar as we accept them. That is, the tolerated others are never just present, they are positioned. Their belonging in the environment in which they come to exist is always a precarious one, for they never exist, they are allowed to exist.

Indigenous women, as virtual strangers at senior levels, are 'outsiders within' (Collins 1991); they have no sense of belonging to a White institution and they frequently cannot find their own space. Hine offered this challenging comment:

> I feel that I am not recognized. I have to remind people in meetings about *karakia* (prayer), I have to remind them about acknowledging new people, about finding how who they are, where they come from ... we seem to be too concerned about process and not about people.

As Aroha explained, leadership was:

> not about talking about what I do. I can't talk myself up. You know what I mean. *Kaore te kūmara e kōrero mo tōna māngaro* [the kumara, or sweet potato, does not talk of its own sweetness]. It's about what I do, how I walk among others, how I walk with others. It's about *wairua* [soul, essence], its about *tangata whenua* [people], it's about *manaakitanga*

[reciprocity], *kaitiakitanga* [guardianship of past, present and future]. And it's about *whanau* [family]. It starts there and goes from there. And comes back to there.

Highlighted here are dimensions of leadership that connect one with the other; the spiritual, the emotional, the physical and the mental. There is no sense of hierarchy, that one is above another based on title or position. Rather, everyone is connected through family and through land. These connections are markedly different from those that operate in the Pākehā or White world where connections are ostensibly based on tradition, privilege and networks.

Attention to diversity as well as broader issues of social justice at any more than a superficial level is risky business precisely because homogeneity invokes a sense of sameness, uniformity and institutional comfort (Fitzgerald 2010). The consistent questioning of White privilege and power (Moreton-Robinson, 2000) is a deafening silence in universities.

The emphasis on individual performance, individual output and individual esteem is contrary to collective values held by Indigenous peoples. If the 'game' of managerialism is a struggle for White women, it is doubly difficult for Indigenous women. 'I have to translate the White language into my own,' said Pat (academic). 'It's what I need to do to be able to understand what is going on.' Located outside of the dominant group (White women and men), Indigenous women struggled to know and understand the dominant organizational values. Myra observed that 'the place is rife with colonization. If I want to get on I have to expose myself. I have to be assimilated into this place. I don't want to be part of that, expose myself, it's just too painful.'

Telling stories

This book has drawn on the life stories of a number of academic and senior women in universities across Australia and New Zealand. The stories recounted are not necessarily common to the whole group. I have not attempted to find common threads but used the stories grounded in women's lives to make sense of how they exercise or experience leadership. The power of these stories is in the everyday talk that marks womens' experiences in the academy.

But this book has not just been about women leaders and women academics, although it is their voices that have percolated through the chapters. Located between the pauses, and between the silences are the observations of what it means to work in a university in the twenty-first century, and the institutional values and practices that dominate the landscape of higher education (Fitzgerald *et al.* 2012). This book is an attempt to understand what it means to be part of the senior management in an environment in which White women are a numerical minority, and Indigenous women are a rare presence. It is at these margins that rich opportunity exists for debate, conflict, agreement/disagreement and potential transformation to occur.

The strong impression that originates from these collective stories is that universities are hostile places for women. Numerous stories have highlighted how women have adjusted to institutional demands and how institutions have failed to respond to their presence and needs. Some women have viewed their career stories in terms of their survival against institutional expectations whereas some women have thrived due in part to the opportunities managerialism has presented. The caveat that exists is that the women leaders portrayed in this book are in elite positions. Despite numerous hurdles and the challenging climate in which their work is situated, nonetheless, as senior women in higher education, they have access to a level of institutional privilege.

For many women there has been a professional and personal cost in being a leader. Long hours, unrelenting expectations and inflexible workplaces and practices have provoked feelings of anger, frustration and inadequacy. Indigenous women frequently commented on their loneliness and isolation, and their continuous struggle to claim a place for themselves in White institutions. Some women resisted attempts to mould themselves to a particular managerial persona, but then felt exposed when their female colleagues did not necessarily support their endeavours. For many their experiences of leadership invariably meant being pushed beyond their limits, to remain in difficult positions as they could see the potential for change, and that their personal and professional lives were intertwined. Mapping these unfolding lives was simultaneously difficult and rewarding as I sought to discover and interpret 'the shape of our creation along the way, rather than pursuing a vision already defined' (Bateson 1989: 1).

Telling their stories was a powerful way for women to ground their own experiences within these narratives. It was an opportunity for women to be active agents in their own lives and their own narratives. Neither teller nor listener was looking for any truths, or right to claim a particular truth. Integral to the telling of one's story was that each woman assigned a level of power and authority to the patterns of their lives and the meanings assigned to those patterns. Their lives were, as Bateson (1989) has contended, both interrupted and conflicted. In composing her life each woman was involved in 'a continual reimagining of the future and reinterpretations of the past to give meaning to the present' (Bateson 1989: 29).

I recognize that in hearing these stories I was assumed to be sympathetic to womens' viewpoints and have a level of understanding of the pleasures and traumas they shared. My own institutional positioning opened up space for me to connect with the women and their stories. Although a research assistant interviewed women at my own institution, many of the women made contact with me to claim their presence in the research. That is, they sought to name themselves as participants or openly commented in other venues about the reflexive opportunities this project had stimulated.

In this book I have integrated components of narrative methodology to move between women's own words (autobiographical) and vignettes of their actions (the everyday) in order to be able to craft a commentary (or interpretation) of women's leadership lives. Drawing on both Bateson (1989) as well as the work of Marshall (1995), the narratives presented represent women's sense-making as well as my own process of making sense of their experiences. I do not claim that these stories are representative and the value and importance of each story lies with the speaker, not the listener or reader. There is no smooth story to tell, no institutional fairy tales to recount. These are stories that are interrupted, partial, amended and incomplete. They are the stories women have told about themselves and about learning to be managers and leaders. These stories disrupt the silences around women leaders and have offered space for women to 'unlearn not to speak' and to reclaim the right to 'talk back' and 'gain a voice' (Marshall 1995: 17).

On reflection, using Bateson's (1989) broad framework has been useful primarily because she encourages lives to be told in discontinuous, multiple and potentially conflicting ways. The temptation is *not* to weave a narrative of a single life story, but to look at the tangled frames and the web of meaning that lie beneath and within the narrative. Drawing out individual life stories was imperative as I was mindful of Bateson's observation that 'the forging of a sense of identity is never finished. Instead it feels like catching one's image reflected in a mirror next to a carousel – "Here I am again"' (Bateson 1989: 219).

For Indigenous women, the opportunity to tell their stories has been an authoritative way to listen to their voices and perspectives and contest their marginality in the academy. By telling their stories, Indigenous women name their realities and their experiences and speak to their relationships and connectedness with the environment and family. But it was not just about what was spoken and heard but what was unspoken. Space was created for silences and, as Hine offered, 'it was in the silence that I began to think. Think about what I could do and think about why I must [act].' These silences are powerful and should not be interrupted. Silence does not permit anyone else to speak but requires individuals to listen to the struggles and consciousness-raising that is occurring (Fitzgerald 2010). Silence can be a liberating act for Indigenous peoples to use to speak back to their fears (Lorde 1984).

The focus then has been on listening to women, not to show how they differ from their male counterparts, but to examine any common ground *between* women. Although many of the women appeared to share common experiences, I have resisted essentialist ways of thinking about women and drawn out contradictions and diversity of experiences. This has left me with a number of questions: How might these stories be repeated, reaffirmed or told differently if women were to collectively share their experiences? Could sharing their stories become a purposeful act of critical reflection and collective action to challenge the institutional status quo? How might connections between women become a powerful mechanism for creating organizational spaces for women?

Creating organizational space

We are at a number of crossroads. First, we are at a numerical crossroads. The statistical picture brings into sharp relief the paucity of women in senior leadership roles in universities. This pattern is replicated across countries and nations such as Australia, the UK, New Zealand, Canada, the USA and Continental Europe (Bagilhole and White 2011; Enders and de Weert 2009; Fitzgerald and Wilkinson 2010; Glazer-Raymo 2008; Ledwith and Manfredi 2000; Morley 2005b). Research has shown that there is a direct correlation between higher productivity and higher levels of gender equity (Bradley 1999; Sagaria 2007). The continued underrepresentation of women at senior levels significantly impacts on the ability of any institution or organization to respond to change (Blackmore and Sachs 2007). Unless there is a rapid rehabilitation of these statistics, the absence of a diversified workforce is a potential threat to the future viability and vitality of institutions and organizations. It is simply not good enough for successful women to take their place alongside successful men. The mark of institutional achievement would be a firm commitment to more equitable outcomes and the dismantling of current regimes of power and privilege. Moreover, unless the filter of Whiteness that underpins these statistics as well as academia more generally is removed, equity *and* diversity will remain an elusive ideal.

Second, we are at a policy crossroads. Despite decades of affirmative action strategies, equity policies and equity employment legislation, the underrepresentation of women in positions of power and authority remains. As the work of Fitzgerald and Wilkinson (2010) and Blackmore and Sachs (2007) has shown, the focus on women as the policy 'problem' will not destabilize the immutable link between masculinity and leadership. Rather than masking or ignoring these complexities and tensions, organizational interventions that engage in practical consciousness-raising to challenge the myriad impacts of links between masculinity and leadership are necessary. Importantly, interventions that bring attention to the impact of gendered discourses and assumptions can challenge the status quo of management. Attention is then fixed on the institution and its gendered systems, structures and processes (Allan 2008; Salisbury and Riddell 2000).

The problem of low numbers of women in senior management is an organizational problem, yet it is rarely cast as such. However dire the statistics appear, there is an emerging trend. That is, numbers of women are increasing however glacial the progress. Ironically, although there has been a disproportionate number of women who have progressed to these senior roles, the policy assumption that has surfaced is that the 'problem' of women's absence from these levels has been resolved (Blackmore 1999; Eveline and Booth 2004; Fitzgerald and Wilkinson 2010). But it is the gendered world itself that represents the problem, not simply the exclusion of women or the continued existence of male norms. Universities can no longer 'turn a deaf ear and a blind eye ... to their organizing principles and processes' (Benschop and Brouns 2003: 195).

Third, we are at a cultural crossroads. Close examination of the impact of new managerialism in higher education (Deem *et al.* 2007; Fitzgerald *et al.* 2012) has exposed the reassertion of the gendered division of labour and a masculinist organizational culture as new regimes of managerial accountabilities, work intensification, the emphasis on productivity and outputs and the close scrutiny and surveillance of staff through performance audits permeate higher education (Collinson and Hearn 1996; Whitehead and Kerfoot 1998). It is this very climate that is discouraging for women insofar as they are reluctant to apply for formal leadership positions (Blackmore and Sachs 2007) due in part to the very nature of the managerial environment that calls for strong entrepreneurial management and individual competitiveness. Indeed, the masculinist culture of higher education (Brooks and Mackinnon 2001; Currie *et al.* 2002) presents women with equally unappealing possibilities: to act as token women or surrogate men or be situated as responsible for challenging the organizational status quo and defend the past gains of gender equity reforms. The potential exists for the 'leadership game' to be reworked or rejected. To this point the implication has been that there is a game to be learned and played and that women are not immediately cognisant of the rules of the game. Those women who do opt to play the leadership game can experience conflict, misunderstanding and disregard from colleagues (Acker 2010). And for some women, playing the game is intensely pleasurable, however arbitrary the rules. But here again a masculinist metaphor has emerged that suggests that there is a game to be played, and that there are 'winners' and 'losers' in this competitive arena. Thinking about leadership as a game may no longer be appropriate.

And we are at a leadership crossroads as, paradoxically, senior women are framed as both academic workers and management workers. As academics they have been highly successful and ascended the academic hierarchy to the level of professor – a title and position that recognizes their scholarly expertise. Roles such as dean, PVC, DVC or VC locate them as managers in the corporatized environment of higher education. As the narratives in this book indicate, women attempt to balance being both an academic and a manager although for many there is a high personal cost in terms of workload, work hours and the fracturing of any work–life balances. The deep ambivalence that exists is that while, on the one hand, women pursue promotion to senior roles, on the other, they are then required to accept the governing rules and values systems. Put simply, women leaders are required to perform and produce (Morley and Walsh 1995), and many women successfully navigate and negotiate these demands.

It is somewhat of an irony that managerialist cultures provoked the possibility that space to exercise leadership in different ways is permissible. As Goode and Bagilhole (1998) have shown, this new economic climate has opened up opportunities for some individual women due in part to their perceived abilities to be collaborative and transparent, establish networks within and across institutions, adopt flexible and responsive approaches to 'client' needs, multi-task and engage in transformational styles of leadership (Due Billing and Alvesson 2000;

Manning 2002). These assumptions about how women lead distort the realities of what it means to be a 'woman' and 'leader' in higher education. However these discourses are read, they do not speak to the everyday experiences of women who have obtained, remained in or vacated leadership roles. Statistical pictures and policy discourses offer a cursory view of the 'problem' but unless there is wider commitment to diversity within and across institutions, leadership in higher education will remain predominantly a male domain.

Each of these four crossroads represents a moment for decisions and changes to be made. Resolving one of the dilemmas may not necessarily alleviate other concerns. For example, the increasing numbers of women at senior levels may address a numerical imbalance but while it appears that women are winning some of these positions their roles appear to be little more than maintenance activities (such as quality assurance, equity and diversity, pastoral care), work that expends a high level of emotional labour (Morley 2005a; Thomas and Davies 2002). It is these tasks of institutional housekeeping (Fitzgerald 2012b) that ultimately take time, space, energy and commitment away from research, publications and the securing of grants, the core ingredients of a productive academic career. The focus on women's under-representation as a policy problem deflects attention away from the managerial environment of higher education that exacerbates inequity and inequitable practices in its tendency to regenerate the unequal distribution of power as well as reinforce patterns of inequality (Blackmore 2003). Underpinning the numerical, policy and organizational dilemmas is the maintenance of masculinist career trajectories (Collinson and Hearn 1994) that solidify male claims to leadership and authority.

The challenge is five-fold. Breaking through gendered structural and cultural barriers to obtain senior roles is the first and immediate challenge. This involves the fracturing of both the vertical and horizontal gendered segregations that exist. Having more women in senior roles by no means guarantees change in culture and attitudes. Women should neither be expected to speak on behalf of women and their collective concerns (Ledwith and Manfredi 2000) nor be solely responsible for keeping gender on the institutional agenda (Fitzgerald and Wilkinson 2010). Precisely because women at senior levels continue to face the challenges of gendered expectations, this as an institutional problem that remains significantly unresolved.

The second challenge is to ensure that women are retained at middle and senior levels and in roles in which leadership, agency and authority can be exercised. It is important then to understand how, why and under what circumstances women reach positions of power in universities. Liff and Ward (2001) argue that many women in middle management do not perceive themselves as being able to reach senior management, given the culture and long hours. Unless this is reconciled, career and family aspirations remain on a collision course.

Understanding the place and space of leadership offers an opportunity to see being a leader and leading as activities grounded in emotion as well as a site for constructing meaning. The power to confer belonging or exclusion can rest with the leader or, as this book has variously shown, with her female colleagues. I am not suggesting that leaders and leadership are romanticized but that a shifting conversation about what it means to be a 'woman' and a 'leader' is required. Instructive here are the voices of Indigenous women who offer ways to think about connections across time, space and place. Thinking about leadership differently requires an abandonment of the discourse of the individual to thinking about ways in which leadership might be a collective venture. At present there is a heavy investment in the sole leader, the one name identifiable in an organizational chart, and leadership as *the* solution to organizational problems (Fitzgerald *et al.* 2012). The challenge is to begin with leadership – leadership that is underpinned by values, ethics, principles and connections and open to multiple meanings and interpretations.

The third challenge is to alleviate the contradictory effect that women's presence at senior levels has created. The time and energy of senior women is corralled either to provide a gender balance on committees (usually in the form of adding one woman to the mix) or to be hyper-visible for gender equality purposes. Women are disadvantaged through these disproportionate expectations as well as confined to particular forms of work based on their gender. Unquestioned is the unambiguous numerical presence of senior men and the uneven dispersal of power and authority.

Benschop and Brouns (2003) have noted that gender imbalances can be perpetuated or even worsened if senior women leave because of job dissatisfaction or to seek alternative opportunities. It might well be the case that senior women have evacuated senior management roles or do not take up appointments at this level because of the gendered nature of the institution or the gendered nature of leadership itself or because the personal and professional contradictions are too exacting. The retreat from senior level roles and responsibilities might well be as a result of women's negative experiences but, longer term, the powerful signal that is relayed to their female colleagues is that securing a senior position is neither professionally nor personally rewarding.

The fourth challenge is to interrogate Whiteness and the concealed White privilege that continues to operate in and across institutions (Blackmore 2010; Lorde 1984). The essential problem still exists – that White is not a colour and those who are White continue to see themselves as colour blind. Bell (2003) has pointed out that these are dangerous fictions as they normalize being White and do not necessarily open up space to interrogate assumptions. In many ways Whiteness and being White have been an unspoken marker of identity. Confronting White privilege is difficult, painful and discomforting but necessary.

The final challenge is to locate a theoretically sophisticated tool to understand the complexities of the positioning of women leaders with regard to exigencies of gender, sexualities, race, class, ethnicity, Indigeneity and spatial location. What is required is a more nuanced understanding of the social relations of gender and how different femininities and masculinities are constructed in relation to each other and in specific contexts. Without this integrated focus, the stories that are told will always be incomplete. The critical questions to ask are: Which women and which men are advantaged/disadvantaged within specific contexts? Which women and which men get to be leaders and why?

Women are powerful actors in their own lives. They have created new intellectual spaces for their ideas and ways of working (Morley 1999, 2013). This project as well as a number of others (see for example Bagilhole and White 2011; Blackmore and Sachs 2007; Fitzgerald 2010; Sinclair 2004) highlight the extent to which women's intellectual, political, creative and activist acumen can be utilized to create different organizational patterns.

Women have the capacity and tenacity to progress and transform university leadership, hierarchies and culture. The power lies in the collective force of women to agitate for change and their refusal to accept the status quo. We have the knowledge, power, capacity and capabilities to build and occupy rooms of our own.

References

Acker, J. (1990) 'Hierarchies, jobs, bodies: A theory of gendered organisations', *Gender and Society*, 4(2): 139–158.

Acker, S. (1994) *Gendered Education: Sociological Reflections on Women, Teaching and Feminism*, Buckingham: Open University Press.

Acker, S. (2010) 'Gendered games in academic leadership', *International Studies in Sociology of Education*, 20(2): 129–152.

Acker, S. (2012) 'Chairing and caring: Gendered dimensions of leadership in academe', *Gender and Education*, 24(4): 411–428.

Acker, S. and Armenti, C. (2004) 'Sleepless in academia', *Gender and Education*, 16(1): 3–24.

Acker, S. and Feuerverger, G. (1996) 'Doing good and feeling bad: The work of women university teachers', *Cambridge Journal of Education*, 26(3): 401–422.

Acker, S. and Feuerverger, G. (1997) 'Enough is never enough: Women's work in academe', in C. Marshall (ed.), *Feminist Critical Policy Analysis II: A Perspective from Post-secondary Education* (pp. 122–140), London: Falmer Press.

Adler, N.J. (1999) 'Global leaders: Women of influence', in G. Powell (ed.), *The Handbook of Gender* (pp. 239–261), Thousand Oaks, CA: Sage.

Adler, S., Laney, J. and Packer, M. (1993) *Managing Women: Feminism and Power in Educational Management*, Buckingham: Open University Press.

Agocs, C. (2002) 'Canada's employment equity legislation and policy 1987–2000: The gap between policy and practice', *International Journal of Manpower*, 23(3): 256–276.

Aisenberg, N. and Harrington, M. (1988) *Women of Academe: Outsiders in the Sacred Grove*, Amherst: University of Massachusetts Press.

Allan, E. (2008). *Policy Discourses, Gender and Education: Constructing Women's Status*, New York: Routledge.

Alvesson, M. (2002) *Understanding Organizational Culture*, London: Sage.

Arya, R. (2012) 'Black feminism in the academy', *Equality, Diversity and Inclusion: An International Journal*, 31(5/6): 556–572.

Association of University Teachers. (2004) *Gender and Research Activity in the 2001 Research Assessment Exercise*, London: Author.

Avis, J. (2002) 'Imaginary friends: Managerialism, globalisation and post-compulsory education and training in England', *Discourse*, 23(1): 75–90.

Bacchi, C. (2004) 'Policy and discourse: Challenging the construction of affirmative action as preferential treatment', *Journal of European Public Policy*, 11(1): 128–146.

Bagilhole, B. (1993) 'Survivors in a male preserve: A study of British women academics' experiences and perceptions of discrimination in a UK university', *Higher Education*, 26: 431–447.

Bagilhole, B. (2000) 'The myth of superman: A feminist investigation of academic careers', paper presented to the 2nd European Conference on Gender Equality in Higher Education, Zurich.

Bagilhole, B. (2007) 'Challenging women in the male academy: Think about draining the swamp', in P. Cotterill, S. Jackson and G. Letherby (eds), *Challenges and Negotiations for Women in Higher Education* (pp. 21–32), Dordrecht, the Netherlands: Springer.

Bagilhole, B. and Goode, J. (2001) 'The contradiction of the myth of individual merit, and the reality of a patriarchal support system in academic careers: A feminist investigation', *European Journal of Women's Studies*, 8(2): 161–180.

Bagilhole, B. and White, K. (2008) 'Toward a gendered skills analysis of senior management positions in UK and Australian universities', *Tertiary Education and Management*, 14(1): 1–12.

Bagilhole, B. and White, K. (eds) (2011) *Gender, Power and Management: A Cross-Cultural Analysis of Higher Education*, New York: Palgrave Macmillan.

Bailyn, L. (2003) 'Academic careers and gender equity: Lessons learned from MIT', *Gender Work and Organization*, 10(2): 137–153.

Bain, O. and Cummings, W. (2000) 'Academe's glass ceiling: Societal, professional, organisational and institutional barriers to the career advancement of academic women', *Comparative Education Review*, 44(4): 493–514.

Baker, M. (2012) *Academic Careers and the Gender Gap*, Vancouver: UBC Press.

Barreto, M. and Ellemers, N. (2010) 'Current issues in the study of social stigma: Some controversies and unresolved issues', *Journal of Social Issues*, 66(3): 431–445.

Barrett, M. (ed.) (1979) *Virginia Woolf, Women and Writing*. New York: Harcourt Brace Jovanovich.

Barry, J., Chandler, J. and Berg, E. (2007) 'Women's movements and the new public management: Higher education in Sweden and England', *Public Administration*, 85(1): 103–122.

Barry, J., Chandler, J. and Clark, H. (2001) 'Between the ivory tower and the academic assembly line', *Journal of Management Studies*, 38(1): 87–101.

Baruch, Y. and Hall, D.T. (2004) 'The academic career: A model for future careers in other sectors?' *Journal of Vocational Behaviour*, 64: 241–262.

Bascia, N. and Young, B. (2001) 'Women's careers beyond the classroom: Changing roles in a changing world', *Curriculum Inquiry*, 31(3): 271–302.

Bateson, M.C. (1989) *Composing a Life*, New York: Atlantic Monthly Press.

Battiste, M. (2000) *Reclaiming Indigenous Voice and Vision*, Seattle: University of Washington Press.

Bell, L.A. (2003) 'Sincere fictions: The pedagogical challenges of preparing white teachers for multicultural classrooms', *Equity and Excellence in Education*, 35(3): 236–244.

Bendl, R. (2008) 'Gender subtexts: Reproduction of exclusion in organizational discourse', *British Journal of Management*, 19: 50–64.

Bendl, R. and Schmidt, A. (2012) 'Revisiting feminist activism at managerial universities', *Equality, Diversity and Inclusion: An International Journal*, 31(5/6): 484–505.

Benschop, Y. and Brouns, M. (2003) 'Crumbling ivory towers: Academic organising and its gender effects', *Gender, Work, and Organisation*, 10(2): 194–212.

Bhabha, H. (1994) *The Location of Culture*, London: Routledge.

Bishop, R. (1998) 'Freeing ourselves from neo-colonial domination in research: A Māori approach to creating knowledge', *Qualitative Studies in Education*, 11(2): 199–219.

Blackmore, J. (1992) 'More power to the powerful: Corporate management, mergers and the implications for women of the reshaping of the "culture" of Australian tertiary education', *Australian Feminist Studies*, 15: 65–89.

Blackmore, J. (1996) 'Doing emotional labour in the educational marketplace: Stories from the field of women in management,' *Discourse*, 17(3): 337–350.

Blackmore, J. (1997) 'Disciplining feminism: A look at gender-equity struggles in Australian higher education', in L.G. Roman and L. Eyre (eds), *Dangerous Territories: Struggles for Difference and Equality in Education* (pp. 75–96), New York and London: Routledge.

Blackmore, J. (1999) *Troubling Women: Feminism, Leadership and Educational Change*, Buckingham: Open University Press.

Blackmore, J. (2003) 'Tracking the nomadic life of the educational researcher: What future for feminist public intellectuals and the performative university?' *The Australian Educational Researcher*, 30(3): 1–24.

Blackmore, J. (2008) 'Anticipating policy and the logics of practice: Australian institutional and academic responses to the globalizing "quality research" agenda', *Access: Critical Perspectives on Communication, Cultural and Policy Studies*, 27(1–2): 97–113.

Blackmore, J. (2009) 'Academic pedagogies, quality logics and performative universities: Evaluating teaching and what students want', *Studies in Higher Education*, 34(8): 857–872.

Blackmore, J. (2010) 'The other within: Race/gender disruptions to the professional learning of white educational leaders', *International Journal of Leadership in Education*, 13(1): 45–61.

Blackmore, J., Brennan, M. and Zipin, L. (eds) (2010) *Re-positioning University Governance and Academic Work*, Rotterdam: Sense Publishers.

Blackmore, J. and Sachs, J. (2000) 'Paradoxes of leadership and management in higher education in times of change: Some Australian reflections', *International Journal of Leadership in Education*, 3(1): 1–16.

Blackmore, J. and Sachs, J. (2007) *Performing and Reforming Leaders: Gender, Educational Restructuring and Organisational Change*, Albany: State University of New York Press.

Blackwell, L. (2001) 'Occupational sex segregation and part-time work in modern Britain', *Gender, Work and Organization*, 8(2): 146–163.

Bown, L. (1999) 'Beyond the degree: Men and women at decision-making levels in British higher education', *Gender and Education*, 11(1): 5–25.

Bradley, H. (1999) *Gender and Power in the Workplace: Analysing the Impact of Economic Change*, London: Macmillan.

Breakwell, G.M. and Tytherleigh, M.Y. (2008) 'UK university leaders at the turn of the 21st century: Changing patterns in their socio-demographic characteristics', *Higher Education*, 56(1): 109–127.

Brooks, A. and Mackinnon, A. (2001) *Gender and the Restructured University: Changing Management and Culture in Higher Education*, Buckingham: Open University Press.

Bryans, P. and Mavin, S. (2003) 'Women learning to be managers: Learning to fit in or to play a different game?' *Management Learning*, 34(1): 111–134.

Bryson, C. (2004) 'What about the workers? The expansion of higher education and the transformation of academic work', *Industrial Relations*, 35(1): 38–57.

Butterwick, S. and Dawson, J. (2005) 'Undone business: Examining the production of academic labour', *Women's Studies International Forum*, 28(1): 51–65.

Calas, M. and Smircich, L. (1993) 'Dangerous liaisons: The "feminine-in-management" meets "globalisation" ', *Business Horizons*, March–April, 71–81.

Carrington, K. and Pratt, A. (2003) *How Far Have We Come? Gender Disparities in the Australian Higher Education System*, Canberra: Department of the Parliamentary Library.

Charles, N. and Davies, C.A (2000) 'Cultural stereotypes and the gendering of senior management', *Sociological Review*, 48(4): 544–567.

Chesterman, C. and Ross-Smith, A. (2006) 'Not tokens: Reaching a "critical mass" of senior women managers', *Employee Relations*, 28(6): 540–552.

Chilisa, B. and Ntseane, G. (2010) 'Resisting dominant discourses: Implications of Indigenous, African feminist theory and methods for gender and education research', *Gender and Education*, 22(6): 617–632.

Clarke, J. and Newman, J. (1993) 'The right to manage: A second managerial revolution', *Cultural Studies*, 7(3): 427–441.

Clarke, J. and Newman, J. (1997) *The Managerial State*, London: Sage.

Clegg, S. and McAuley, J. (2005) 'Conceptualising middle management in higher education: A multifaceted discourse', *Journal of Higher Education Policy and Management*, 27(1): 19–34.

Cohn, S. (2000) *Race, Gender and Discrimination at Work*, Boulder, CO: Westview Press.

Coleman, M. (2011) *Women at the Top: Challenges, Choices and Change*, New York: Palgrave Macmillan.

Collins, P. (1991) *Black Feminist Thought: Knowledge, Consciousness and the Politics of Empowerment*, New York: Routledge.

Collins, P. (1998) *Fighting Words: Black Women and the Search for Justice*, Minneapolis: University of Minnesota Press.

Collinson, D. and Hearn, J. (1994) 'Naming men as men: Implications for work, organisation and management', *Gender, Work and Organization*, 1(1): 2–22.

Collinson, D. and Hearn, J. (1996) *Managers as Men: Critical Perspectives on Men, Masculinities and Managements*, London: Sage.

Connell, R.W. (1995) *Masculinities*, Sydney: Allen and Unwin.

Connell, R. (2006) 'The experience of gender change in public sector organisations', *Gender, Work and Organization*, 13(5): 435–452.

Corsun, D.L. and Costen, W.M. (2001) 'Is the glass ceiling unbreakable? Habitus, fields and the stalling of women and minorities in management', *Journal of Management Inquiry*, 10(1): 16–25.

Cotterill, P., Jackson, S. and Letherby, G. (2007) *Challenges and Negotiations for Women in Higher Education*, Dordrecht: Springer.

Currie, J., Thiele, B. and Harris, P. (2002) *Gendered Universities in Globalized Economies: Power, Careers, and Sacrifices*, Lanham, MD: Lexington Books.

Dace, K.L. (ed.) (2012) *Unlikely Allies: Women of Colour and White Women in Conversation*, Abingdon: Routledge.

Darwin, A. (2000) 'Critical reflections on mentoring in work settings', *Adult Education Quarterly*, 50(3): 197–211.

David, M. and Woodward, D. (eds) (1998) *Negotiating the Glass Ceiling: Careers of Senior Women in the Academic World*, London: Falmer Press.

Davidson, M.J. (1997) *The Black and Ethnic Minority Manager: Cracking the Concrete Ceiling*, London: Paul Chapman.

Davidson, M.J. and Burke, R.J. (eds) (2000) *Women in Management: Current Research Issues*, London: Sage.

Davidson, M.J. and Cooper, C.L (1992) *Shattering the Glass Ceiling: The Woman Manager*, London: Paul Chapman Publishing.

Davies, B., Gottsche, M. and Bansel, P. (2006) 'The rise and fall of the neoliberal university', *European Journal of Education*, 41(2): 305–319.

Davis, K. (2008) 'Intersectionality as buzzword: A sociology of science perspective on what makes a feminist theory successful', *Feminist Theory*, 9(1): 67–85.

Deem, R. (2001) 'Globalisation, new managerialism, academic capitalism and entrepreneurialism in universities: Is the local dimension still important?', *Comparative Education*, 37(1): 7–20.

Deem, R. (2003) 'Gender, organizational cultures and the practices of manager-academics in UK universities', *Gender, Work and Organization*, 10(2): 239–259.

Deem, R. (2004) 'The knowledge worker, the manager-academic and the contemporary UK university: New and old forms of public management?' *Financial Accountability and Management*, 20(2): 107–128.

Deem, R. and Brehony, K. (2005) 'Management as ideology: The case of "new managerialism" in higher education', *Oxford Review of Education*, 31(2): 217–235.

Deem, R. and Ozga, J. (2000) 'Transforming post-compulsory education? Femocrats at work in the academy', *Women's Studies International Forum*, 23(2): 153–166.

Deem, R., Hillyard, S. and Reed, M. (2007) *Knowledge, Higher Education, and the New Managerialism: The Changing Management of UK Universities*, Oxford: Oxford University Press.

Derks, B., Ellemers, N., van Laar, C. and de Groot, K. (2011) 'Do sexist organizational cultures create the Queen Bee?' *British Journal of Social Psychology*, 50(3): 519–535.

Devine, D., Grummell, B. and Lynch, K. (2011) 'Crafting the elastic self? Gender and identities in senior appointments in Irish education', *Gender, Work and Organization*, 18(6): 631–649.

Devos, A. (2005) 'Mentoring, women and the construction of academic identities', unpublished doctoral thesis, Faculty of Education, University of Technology, Sydney.

Devos, A. (2008) 'Where enterprise and equity meet: The rise of mentoring for women in Australian universities', *Discourse: Studies in the Cultural Politics of Education*, 29 (2): 195–205.

De Vries, J. (2005) *More than the Sum of Its Parts: Ten Years of the Leadership Development for Women Programme at UWA*, Perth: UWA.

Doherty, L. and Manfredi, S. (2006) 'Women's progression to senior positions in English universities', *Employee Relations*, 28(6): 553–572.

Ducklin, A. and Ozga, J. (2007) 'Gender and management in further education in Scotland: An agenda for research', *Gender and Education*, 19(5): 627–646.

Due Billing, Y. (2011) 'Are women in management victims of the phantom male norm?' *Gender, Work and Organization*, 18(3): 298–317.

Due Billing, Y. and Alvesson, M. (2000) 'Questioning the notion of feminine leadership: A critical perspective on the gender labelling of leadership', *Gender, Work and Organisation*, 7(3): 144–157.

Durbin, S. and Tomlinson, J. (2010) 'Female part-time managers: Networks and career mobility', *Work, Employment and Society*, 24(4): 621–640.

Eagly, A.H. and Carli, L.L. (2007) *Through the Labyrinth: The Truth about How Women Become Leaders*, Boston: Harvard Business School.

Eagly, A., Makhijani, M.G. and Klonsky, B.G. (1992) 'Gender and the evaluation of leaders', *Psychological Bulletin*, 111: 3–22.

Eggins, H. (1997) *Women as Leaders and Managers in Higher Education*, Buckingham: Open University Press.

Eisenstein, H. (1996) *Inside Agitators: Australian Femocrats and the State*, Philadelphia: Temple University Press.

Ellis, K. (2011) 'Celebrating 100 years of International Women's Day: Where to from here?' Speech delivered at the National Press Club (Canberra), 9 March 2011; www.kateellis.fahcsia.gov.au/speeches/Pages/celebrating_100_yrs_int_women_09032011.aspx; accessed 8 August 2012.

Ely, R.J. and Meyerson, D.E. (2000) 'Theories of gender in organizations: A new approach to organizational analyses and change', *Research in Organizational Behaviour*, 22: 103–151.

Ely, R., Foldy, E.G. and Scully, M. (eds) (2003) *Reader in Gender, Work and Organization*, Oxford: Blackwell.

Enders, J. and de Weert, E. (eds) (2009) *The Changing Face of Academic Life: Analytical and Comparative Perspectives*, New York: Palgrave Macmillan.

Essed, P. (2000) 'Dilemmas in leadership: Colour in the academy', *Ethnic and Racial Studies*, 23(5): 888–904.

Eveline, J. (2004) *Ivory Basement Leadership: Power and Invisibility in the Changing University*, Crawley: University of Western Australia Press.

Eveline, J. (2005) 'Woman in the ivory tower: Gendering feminized and masculinized identities', *Journal of Organizational Change Management*, 18(6): 641–658.

Eveline, J. and Booth, M. (2004) 'Don't write about it: Writing the "other" for the ivory basement', *Journal of Organizational Change Management*, 17(3): 243–255.

Exworthy, M. and Halford, S. (eds) (1999) *Professionals and the New Managerialism in the Public Sector*, Buckingham: Open University Press.

Fagenson, E. (ed.) (1993) *Women in Management: Trends, Issues and Challenges in Managerial Diversity*, Thousand Oaks, CA: Sage.

Fee, M. and Russell, L. (2007) '"Whiteness" and "Aboriginality" in Canada and Australia: Conversations and identity', *Feminist Theory* 8(2): 187–208.

Fitzgerald, T. (2009) *Outsiders or Equals: Women Professors at the University of New Zealand 1911–1961*. Oxford: Peter Lang.

Fitzgerald, T. (2010) 'Spaces in-between: Indigenous women leaders speak back', *International Journal of Leadership in Education*, 13(1): 93–105.

Fitzgerald, T. (2012a) 'Tracing the fault lines', in T. Fitzgerald, J. White and H.M. Gunter. *Hard Labour? Academic Work and the Changing Landscape of Higher Education* (pp. 1–22), Bingley, UK: Emerald.

Fitzgerald, T. (2012b) 'Ivory basements and ivory towers', in T. Fitzgerald, J. White and H.M. Gunter. *Hard Labour? Academic Work and the Changing Landscape of Higher Education* (pp. 113–135), Bingley, UK: Emerald.

Fitzgerald, T. and Wilkinson, J. (2010) *Travelling Towards a Mirage? Gender, Leadership and Higher Education*, Brisbane: Post Pressed.

Fitzgerald, T., White, J. and Gunter, H.M. (2012) *Hard Labour? Academic Work and the Changing Landscape of Higher Education*, Bingley, UK: Emerald.

Fletcher, J.K. (2004) 'The paradox of postheroic leadership: An essay on gender, power and transformational change', *Leadership Quarterly*, 15: 647–661.

Fournier, V. and Kelemen, M. (2001) 'The crafting of community: Recoupling discourses of management and womanhood', *Gender, Work and Organization*, 8(3): 267–290.

Gallop, J. (ed.) (1995) *Pedagogy: The Question of Impersonation*, Bloomington: Indiana University Press.

Garcia-Retamero, R. and Lopez-Zafra, E. (2006) 'Prejudice against women in male-congenial environments: Perceptions of gender role congruity in leadership', *Sex Roles*, 55: 51–61.

Gherardi, S. (1996) 'Gendered organisational cultures: Narratives of women travelers in a male world', *Gender, Work and Organization*, 3(4): 187–201.

Gherardi, S. and Poggio, B. (2007) *Gendertelling in Organizations: Narratives from Male-Dominated Environments*, Stockholm: Copenhagen Business School Press.

Gibson, S.K. (2006) 'Mentoring of women faculty: The role of organizational politics and culture', *Innovative Higher Education*, 31(1): 63–79.

Gini, A. (2001) *My Job, My Self: Work and the Creation of the Modern Individual*. London: Routledge.

Glazer-Raymo. J. (1999) *Shattering the Myths: Women in Academe*, Baltimore, MD: Johns Hopkins University Press.

Glazer-Raymo, J. (ed.) (2008) *Unfinished Agendas: New and Continuing Gender Challenges in Higher Education*, Baltimore, MD: Johns Hopkins University Press.

Goode, J. and Bagilhole, B. (1998) 'Gendering the management of change in higher education: A case study', *Gender, Work and Organization*, 5(3): 148–164.

Grummell, B., Devine, D. and Lynch, K. (2009) 'The care-less manager: Gender, care and new managerialism in higher education', *Gender and Education*, 21(2), 191–208.

Guillaume, C. and Pochic, S. (2009) 'What would you sacrifice? Access to top management and work–life balance', *Gender, Work and Organization*, 16(1): 14–36.

Gumport, P. (2000) 'Academic restructuring: Organisational change and institutional imperatives', *Higher Education Quarterly*, 39, 67–91.

Hall, V. (1996) *Dancing on the Ceiling: A Study of Woman Managers in Education*, London: Paul Chapman Publishing.

Hage, G. (1994) 'Locating multiculturalisms other: A critique of practical tolerance', *New Formations*, 24(1): 19–34.

Hakim, C. (2000) *Work–Lifestyle Choices in the Twenty-first Century: Preference Theory*, Oxford: Oxford University Press.

Halvorsen, E. (2002) 'Female academics in a knowledge production society', *Higher Education Quarterly*, 56(4): 347–359.

Hansard Society Commission (1990) *Women at the Top*, London: The Hansard Society for Parliamentary Government.

Haslam, S.A. and Ryan, M.K. (2008) 'The road to the glass cliff: Differences in the perceived suitability of men and women for leadership positions in succeeding and failing organizations', *Leadership Quarterly*, 19: 530–546.

Hatcher, C. (2003) 'Refashioning a passionate manager: Gender at work', *Gender, Work and Organization*, 10(4): 391–411.

Haywood, S. (2005) *Women Leading*, Basingstoke: Palgrave Macmillan.

Hazelkorn, E. (2011) *Rankings and the Reshaping of Higher Education: The Battle for World-class Excellence*, New York: Palgrave Macmillan.

Henry, E. and Pringle, J. (1996) 'Making voices, being heard in Aotearoa/New Zealand', *Organization*, 3(4): 534–540.

Heward, C. (1999) 'Equal opportunities in the professions: A research agenda', *Research Papers in Education*, 14(1): 79–92.

Hey, V. and Bradford, S. (2004) 'The return of the repressed? The gender politics of emergent forms of professionalism in education', *Journal of Education Policy*, 19(6): 691–713.

Higher Education Statistics Agency. (2013) HESA homepage. Available at www.hesa.ac.uk.

hooks, b. (1989) *Talking Back: Thinking Feminist – Thinking Black*, Boston: South End Press.

Höpfl, H. and Matilal, S. (2007) 'The lady vanishes: Some thoughts on women and leadership', *Journal of Organisational Change Management*, 20(2): 198–208.

Hughes, C. (2000) 'Is it possible to be a feminist manager in the "real world" of further education?' *Journal of Further and Higher Education*, 24(2): 251–260.

Hughes, C. (2004) 'Class and other identifications in managerial careers: The case of the lemon dress', *Gender, Work and Organization*, 11(5): 526–543.

Husu, L. (2001) *Sexism, Support and Survival in Academia: Academic Women and Hidden Discrimination in Finland*, Helsinki: University of Helsinki Press.

Itzen, C. and Newman, J. (1995) *Gender, Culture and Organizational Change: Putting Theory into Practice*, Abingdon: Routledge.

Jenkins, R. (1996) *Social Identity*, London: Routledge.

Jones, D. (2004) 'Screwing diversity out of the workers? Reading diversity', *Journal of Organisational Change Management*, 17(3): 281–291.

Kanter, R. (1993) *Men and Women of the Corporation*, 2nd edition, New York: Basic Books.

Keller, E.F. and Moglen, H. (1987) 'Competition and feminism: Conflicts for women academics', *Signs*, 12: 493–511.

Kerfoot, D. and Knights, D. (1993) 'Management, manipulation and masculinity: From paternalism to corporate strategy in financial services', *Journal of Management Studies*, 30(4): 659–677.

Kerfoot, D. and Knights, D. (1996) *Men as Managers, Managers as Men: Critical Perspectives on Men, Masculinites and Managements*, London: Sage.

Kerfoot, D. and Knights, D. (2004) *Management, Organization and Masculinity*, London: Sage.

Kimber, M. (2003) 'The tenured "core" and the tenuous "periphery": The casualisation of academic work in Australian universities', *Journal of Higher Education Policy and Management*, 25(1): 41–50.

Kloot, L. (2004) 'Women and leadership in universities: A case study of women academic managers', *International Journal of Public Sector Management*, 17(6): 470–485.

Knights, D. and Kerfoot, D. (2004) 'Between representations and subjectivity: Gender binaries and the politics of organisational transformation', *Gender, Work and Organization*, 11(4): 430–454.

Kram, K. and McCollom Hampton, M. (2003) 'When women lead: The visibility–vulnerability spiral', in R. Ely, E.G. Foldy and M. Scully (eds), *Reader in Gender, Work and Organization* (pp. 211–223), Oxford: Blackwell.

Lafferty, G. and Fleming, J. (2000) 'The restructuring of academic work in Australia: Power, management and gender', *British Journal of Sociology of Education*, 21(2): 257–267.

Leathwood, C. (2000) 'Happy families: Pedagogy, management and parental discourses of control in the corporatized further education college', *Journal of Further and Higher Education*, 24(2): 163–182.

Leathwood, C. and Read, B. (2009) *Gender and the Changing Face of Higher Education: A Feminised Future?* Maidenhead: SRHE/Open University Press.

Ledwith, S. and Manfredi, S. (2000) 'Balancing gender in higher education: A study of the experience of senior women in a "new" UK university', *European Journal of Women's Studies*, 7: 7–33.

Leonard, P. (1998) 'Gendering change? Management, masculinity and the dynamics of incorporation', *Gender and Education*, 10(1): 71–84.

Lester, J. (2008) 'Performing gender in the workplace: Gender socialization, power, and identity among women faculty members', *Community College Review*, 35(4): 277–305.

Lewis, K. (2000) 'When leaders display emotion: How followers respond to negative emotional expression of male and female leaders', *Journal of Organizational Behaviour*, 21(2): 221–234.

Liff, S. and Ward, K. (2001) 'Distorted views through the glass ceiling: The construction of women's understandings of their promotion and senior management positions', *Gender, Work and Organization*, 8(1): 19–35.

Lorde, A. (ed.) (1984) *Sister Outsider*. Trumansburg, NY: Crossing Press.

Lucashenko, M. (1994) 'No other truth? Aboriginal women and Australian feminists', *Social Alternatives*, 12(4): 21–24.

Luke, C. (2001) *Globalization and Women in Academia: North/west–south/east*, Abingdon: Routledge.

McCarthy, H. (2004) *Girlfriends in High Places*, London: Demos.

McIntosh, P. (1985) *Feeling Like a Fraud*, Wellesley, MA: Stone Center for Developmental Services and Studies.

McKeen, C. and Bujaki, M. (2007) 'Gender and mentoring', in B.R. Ragins and K.K. Kram (eds), *Handbook of Mentoring at Work: Theory, Research and Practice* (pp. 197–222), Thousand Oaks, CA: Sage.

McTavish, D. and Miller, K. (eds) (2006) *Women in Leadership and Management*, Cheltenham: Edward Elgar.

McTavish, D. and Miller, K. (2007) *Gender Balance in Management: Higher and Further Education Sectors in Scotland*, Glasgow: Caledonian University.

McTavish, D. and Miller, K. (2009) 'Management, leadership and gender representation in UK higher and further education', *Gender in Management: An International Journal*, 24(3): 178–194.

Maddock, S. (1999) *Challenging Women: Gender, Culture and Organisation*, London: Sage.

Madsen, S.R. (2008) *On Becoming a Woman Leader: Learning from the Experiences of University Presidents*, San Francisco: Jossey-Bass.

Maher, F.A. and Tetreault, M.K.T. (2007) *Privilege and Diversity in the Academy*, New York: Routledge.

Mama, A. (2003) 'Restore, reform but do not transform: the gender politics of higher education in Africa', *Journal of Higher Education in Africa*, 1: 101–125.

Manning, T. (2002) 'Gender, managerial level, transformational leadership and work satisfaction', *Women in Management Review*, 17(5): 207–216.

Maranto, C. and Griffin, A. (2011) 'The antecedents of a "chilly climate" for women faculty in higher education', *Human Relations*, 64(2): 139–159.

Marginson, S. (2000) 'Rethinking academic work in the global era', *Journal of Higher Education Policy and Management*, 22(1): 23–35.

Marshall, J. (1984) *Women Managers: Travellers in a Male World*, London: Wiley.

Marshall, J. (1995) *Women Managers Moving On: Exploring Career and Life Choices*, London: Routledge.

Martin, P.Y. (2006) 'Practising gender at work: Further thoughts on reflexivity', *Gender, Work and Organization*, 13(3): 254–276.

Mauthner, N. and Edwards, R. (2010) 'Feminist research management in higher education in Britain: Possibilities and practices', *Gender, Work and Organization*, 17(5): 481–502.

Mavin, S. (2006) 'Venus envy 2: Sisterhood, queen bees and female misogyny in management', *Women in Management Review*, 21(5): 349–364.

Mavin, S. (2008) 'Queen bees, wannabees and afraid to bees: No more "best enemies" for women in management?' *British Journal of Management*, 19: S75–S84.

Mavin, S. and Bryans, P. (2002) 'Academic women in the UK: Mainstreaming our experiences and networking for action', *Gender and Education*, 14(3): 235–250.

Mavin, S. and Grandy, G. (2012) 'Doing gender well and differently in management', *Gender in Management: An International Journal*, 27(4): 218–231.

May, T. (2005) 'Transformations in academic production: Content, context and consequences', *European Journal of Social Theory*, 8(2): 193–209.

Metcalfe, A.S. and Slaughter, S. (2008) 'The differential effects of academic capitalism on women in the academy', in J. Glazer-Raymo (ed.), *Unfinished Agendas: New and Continuing Gender Challenges in Higher Education* (pp. 80–111), Baltimore, MD: Johns Hopkins University Press.

Meyerson, D. (2001) *Tempered Radicals: How Everyday Leaders Inspire Change at Work*, Cambridge, MA: Harvard University Press.

Meyerson, D.E. and Scully, M.A. (1995) 'Tempered radicalism and the politics of ambivalence and change', *Organization Science*, 6(5): 585–600.

Meyerson, D.E. and Tompkins, M. (2007) 'Tempered radicals as institutional change agents: the case of advancing gender equity at the University of Michigan', *Harvard Journal of Law and Gender*, 30(2): 303–322.

Miller, K. (2006) 'Introduction: Women in leadership and management: Progress thus far?' in D. McTavish and K. Miller (eds), *Women in Leadership and Management* (pp. 1–10), Cheltenham: Edward Elgar.

Miller, N. and Morgan, D. (1993) 'Called to account: The CV as an autobiographical practice', *Sociology*, 27(1): 133–143.

Miner, V. and Longino, H.E. (eds) (1987) *Competition: A Feminist Taboo?* New York: The Feminist Press.

Morley, L. (1999) *Organising Feminisms: The Micropolitics of the Academy*, Basingstoke: Macmillan.

Morley, L. (2001) 'Producing new workers: Quality, equality and employability in higher education', *Quality in Higher Education*, 7(2): 131–138.

Morley, L. (2003) *Quality and Power in Higher Education*, Buckingham: Open University Press.

Morley, L. (2005a) 'Opportunity or exploitation? Women and quality assurance in higher education', *Gender and Education*, 17(4): 411–429.

Morley, L. (2005b) 'Sounds, silences and contradictions: Gender equity in British Commonwealth higher education', *Australian Feminist Studies*, 20(46): 109–119.

Morley, L. (2013) 'The rules of the game: Women and the leaderist turn in higher educa-tion', *Gender and Education*, 25(1): 116–131.

Morley, L. and Walsh, V. (1995) *Feminist Academics: Creative Agents for Change*, London: Taylor and Francis.

Morley, L. and Walsh, V. (eds) (1996) *Breaking Boundaries: Women in Higher Educa-tion*, London: Taylor and Francis.

Moreton-Robinson, A. (2000) *Talkin' Up to the White Women: Indigenous Women and Feminism*, St Lucia: University of Queensland Press.

Mumford, R. and Rumball, S. (1999) 'Women, culture and powersharing', unpublished seminar paper, Massey University, New Zealand.

Ng, C.W. and Chiu, W.C.K. (2001) 'Managing equal opportunities for women: Sorting the friends from the foes', *Human Resource Management Journal*, 11(1): 75–88.

Noble, C. and Moore, S. (2006) 'Advancing women and leadership in this post feminist, post EEO era: A discussion of the issues', *Women in Management Review*, 21(7): 598–603.

O'Connor, P. (2008) 'The challenge of gender in higher education: Processes and prac-tices', *Proceedings of the 4th International Barcelona Conference on Higher Education*, vol. 3, *Higher Education and Gender Equity*. Barcelona: GUNI.

Olssen, S. (2000) 'Acknowledging the female archetype: Women managers' narratives of gender', *Women in Management Review*, 15(5/6): 296–302.

Park, S.M. (1996) 'Research, teaching, service: Why shouldn't women's work count?' *Journal of Higher Education*, 67(1): 46–84.

Parks-Stamm, E.H., Heilman, M.E. and Hearns, K.A. (2008) 'Motivated to penalize: Women's strategic rejection of successful women', *Personality and Social Psychology Bulletin*, 34(2): 237–247.

Perriton, L. (2006) 'Does woman + career = career progression?' *Leadership*, 2(1): 101–113.

Peterson, H. (2011) 'The gender mix policy: Addressing gender inequality in higher education management', *Journal of Higher Education Policy and Management*, 33(6): 619–628.

Prichard, C. and Deem, R. (1999) 'Wo-managing further education: Gender and the construction of the manager in the corporate colleges of England', *Gender and Educa-tion*, 11(3): 323–342.

Priola, V. (2007) 'Being female doing gender: Narratives of women in education man-agement', *Gender and Education*, 19(1): 21–40.

Probert, B. (2005) '"I just couldn't fit it in": Gender and unequal outcomes in academic careers', *Gender, Work and Organization*, 12(1): 50–72.

Probert, B., Ewer, P. and Whiting, K. (1998) *Gender Pay Equity in Australian Higher Education*, Melbourne: NTEU.

Raddon, A. (2002) 'Mothers in the academy', *Studies in Higher Education*, 27(4): 387–403.

Reay, D. (2000) 'Dim dross: Marginalised women both inside and outside the academy', *Women's Studies International Forum*, 23(1): 13–21.

Rhode. D.L. (ed.) (2003) *The Difference 'Difference' Makes: Women and Leadership*, Stanford, CA: Stanford University Press.

Richardson, L. (1997) *Fields of Play: Constructing an Academic Life*, New Brunswick, NJ: Rutgers University Press.

Roman, L.G. and Eyre, L. (eds) (1997) *Dangerous Territories: Struggles for Difference and Equality in Education*. New York and London: Routledge.

Rose, H. (1998) 'An accidental academic', in M. David and D. Woodward (eds),

Negotiating the Glass Ceiling: Careers of Senior Women in the Academic World (pp. 101–113), London: Falmer Press.

Ross-Smith, A. and Chesterman, C. (2009) 'Girl disease: Women managers' reticence and ambivalence towards organizational advancement', *Journal of Management and Organization*, 15(5): 582–595.

Ryan, M. and Haslam, S. (2005) 'The glass cliff: Evidence that women are over-represented in precarious leadership positions', *British Journal of Management*, 16(2): 81–90.

Ryan, M., Haslam, A. and Postmes, T. (2007) 'Reactions to the glass cliff: Gender differences in the explanations for the precariousness of women's leadership positions', *Journal of Organizational Change and Management*, 20(2): 182–197.

Sagaria, M.A (2007) *Women, Universities and Change: Gender Equality in the European Union and the United States*, New York: Palgrave Macmillan.

Salisbury, J. and Riddell, S. (eds) (2000) *Gender, Policy and Educational Change: Shifting Agendas in the UK and Europe*, London: Routledge.

Saunderson, W. (2002) 'Women, academia and identity: Constructions of equal opportunities in the "new managerialism" – a case of lipstick on the gorilla?' *Higher Education Quarterly*, 56(4): 376–406.

Schein, V.E. (2007) 'Women in management: reflections and projections', *Women in Management Review*, 22(1): 6–18.

Schein, V.E. and Davidson, M.J. (1993) 'Think manager, think male', *Management Development Review*, 6(3): 24–28.

Schnurr, S. (2008) 'Surviving in a man's world with a sense of humour: An analysis of women leaders' use of humour at work', *Leadership*, 4(3): 299–320.

Siemieñska, R. and Zimmer, A. (eds) (2007) *Gendered Career Trajectories in Academia in Cross-National Perspective*, Warsaw: Wydawnictwo Naukowe Scholar.

Sinclair, A. (1998) *Doing Leadership Differently: Gender, Power and Sexuality in a Changing Business Culture*, Melbourne: Melbourne University Press.

Sinclair, A. (2004) 'Journey around leadership', *Discourse: Studies in the Cultural Politics of Education*, 25(1): 7–19.

Sinclair, A. and Wilson, V. (2002) *New Faces of Leadership*, Melbourne: Melbourne University Press.

Skelton, C. (2005) 'The "self-interested" woman academic: A consideration of Beck's model of the "individualized individual"', *British Journal of Sociology of Education*, 26(1): 5–16.

Slaughter, S. and Rhoades, G. (2004) *Academic Capitalism and the New Economy: Markets, State and Higher Education*, Baltimore, MD: Johns Hopkins University Press.

Smith, D. (1990) *The Conceptual Practices of Power: A Feminist Sociology of Knowledge*, Boston: Northeastern University Press.

Swan, E. and Fox, S. (2010) 'Playing the game: Strategies of resistance and co-optation in diversity work', *Gender, Work and Organization*, 9(4): 372–397.

Thomas, R. and Davies, A. (2002) 'Gender and the new public management: Reconstituting academic subjectivities', *Gender, Work and Organization*, 9(4): 372–397.

Thornton, M. (2000) *Nexus*, 10(2), July.

Wagner, I. and Wodak, R. (2006) 'Performing success: Identifying strategies of self-presentation in women's biographical narratives', *Discourse and Society*, 17(3): 385–411.

Wajcman, J. (1998) *Managing Like a Man: Women and Men in Corporate Management*, Cambridge: Polity Press.

West, C. and Zimmerman, D. (1987) 'Doing gender', *Gender and Society*, 1(2): 125–151.

White, K. (2001) 'Women in the professoriate in Australia', *International Journal of Organisational Behaviour*, 3(2): 64–76.

White, K. (2003) 'Women and leadership in higher education in Australia', *Tertiary Education and Management*, 9(1): 45–60.

White, K. (2004) 'The leaking pipeline: Women postgraduate and early career researchers in Australia', *Tertiary Education and Management*, 10(3): 227–241.

White, K., Carvalho, T. and Riordan, S. (2011) 'Gender, power and managerialism in universities', *Journal of Higher Education Policy and Management*, 33(2): 179–188.

Whitehead, S. (1998) 'Disrupted selves: Resistance and identity work in the managerial arena', *Gender and Education*, 10(2): 199–215.

Whitehead, S. and Kerfoot, D. (1998) 'Boy's own stuff: Masculinity and the management of further education', *Sociological Reviews*, 46(3): 436–457.

Williams, C. (1992) 'The glass escalator: Hidden advantages for men in the "female" professions', *Social Problems*, 39(3): 253–267.

Wilson, F. (1996) 'Research note: Organizational theory – blind and deaf to gender', *Organization Studies*, 17(5): 825–842.

Wilson, F. (2005) 'Caught between difference and similarity: The case of women academics', *Women in Management Review*, 20(4): 234–248.

Woolf, V. (1957). *The Death of the Moth and Other Essays*. London: Hogarth Press.

Wyn, J., Acker, S. and Richards, E. (2000) 'Making a difference: Women in management in Australian and Canadian faculties of education', *Gender and Education*, 12(4): 435–444.

Index